THE CAST IRON SKILLET COOKBOOK

THE CAST IRON SKILLET COOKBOOK

Recipes for the Best Pan in Your Kitchen

SHARON KRAMIS & JULIE KRAMIS HEARNE

SASQUATCH BOOKS
SEATTLE

For Elsie—mother, grandmother, and great-grandmother—

who inspired us to continue cooking in the cast iron skillet.

—S. K. and J. K. H.

Printed in Canada
Published by Sasquatch Books
Distributed by Publishers Group West
12 11 10 09   14 13 12 11 10

Photography: Alex Hayden
Book design: Kate Basart

Library of Congress Cataloging-in-Publication Data

Kramis, Sharon.
     The cast iron skillet cookbook : recipes for the best pan in your kitchen /
     Sharon Kramis and Julie Kramis Hearne.
          p. cm.
     ISBN 1-57061-425-3
     1. Skillet cookery. 2. Cast-iron. I. Hearne, Julie Kramis. II. Title.

TX840.S55K73 2004
641.7'7--dc22   2004046736

Sasquatch Books / 119 South Main Street, Suite 400 / Seattle, WA 98104 / (206) 467-4300
www.sasquatchbooks.com / custserv@sasquatchbooks.com

CONTENTS

To my darling daughter Julie, who loves to cook. We have so much fun sharing food experiences together. To my husband, Larry, who was our food critic. To Joe Kramis, and Tom Kramis and his family, who appreciate gathering together to cook and share good food. Thanks, Dad, for

ACKNOWLEDGMENTS

always making me try something new. And a very special thanks to Marion Cunningham, who invites everyone to the table for a memorable meal. To all of our friends at Anthony's Restaurants with respect and appreciation for your commitment to quality and community. —S. K.

To my co-author, mom, and friend, who took me through the looking glass into the wonderful world of food. A special thanks to my supportive husband, Harker, and my little taste testers, Reilly and Konrad. —J. K. H.

Both authors would like to thank our editor, Janet Kimball, for helping to bring this book to fruition. Our thanks to Gary Luke, Chad Haight, and everyone at Sasquatch Books for believing in us and the cast iron skillet. A special thanks to Alex Hayden, our photographer, who brought these recipes to life, and Christy Nordstrom, our food stylist, who made everything look as good as it tastes. —S. K. and J. K. H.

A Note to Our Readers

In our family, we are part of three generations of women who have been cooking side by side for many years. We love to cook. We can always be found shopping for food, cooking food, talking about food, or reading food magazines. Our favorite outing is a visit to our local farmers market. We load up our baskets and plan our menu for that night's dinner. It's our passion, and we discover something new each time we cook, usually in the cast iron skillet. We hope you will rescue your cast iron skillet from the garage or back cupboard and enjoy the sounds and smells of cooking the recipes in this book.

It's a wonderful thing to step into a friend's kitchen and see a cast iron skillet on the stove. You know right then that you are going to have something good to eat, that you are in the home of a true cook. A cast iron skillet has an heirloom quality about it. Every pan has its own stories to tell, memories of sharing good food with friends and loved ones. No other pan has this kind of history. Passed from generation to generation, old cast iron skillets remind our senses of smells and flavors that make us want to heat them up and hear them sizzle with good food again.

The cast iron skillet is one of the most important pans in your kitchen. It is the key to good cooking. We'll admit up front that a cast iron skillet is heavy and a bit more difficult to clean and maintain than a skillet coated with Teflon or other nonstick material. So why use it? For browning, searing, roasting, and caramelizing, we have greater success with cast iron

INTRODUCTION

than with any other kind of pan. Certain recipes require an iron skillet; others just taste better when cooked in one. Cast iron's unique characteristic of producing dry, even heat makes it ideal for baking as well. Baked goods come out moist on the inside with a crisp, golden crust on the outside. Vegetables roast and caramelize perfectly. Meats sear and brown just as they should and don't seize up or stew, because cast iron doesn't cause additional moisture to form.

For four generations the cast iron skillet has played an important role in our family. Sunday mornings always meant peeking into the oven to watch the Dutch baby rise, the sautéed apples and powdered sugar waiting on the table. We've included many of our favorite recipes that have been in our family for years. Our well-seasoned cast iron skillets connect our family history with love, one generation to the next.

Here we present to you good food, done well. Along with our classic family favorites you will find adventurous new dishes with ingredients that bring together flavors from around the world. You will find recipes that are timeless and versatile, and cooking them in cast iron makes all the difference. If in the past you have prepared a dish similar to one of these in another kind of pan, try it in cast iron.

The cast iron skillet is the reason cooks are making tarte Tatin in France, tortilla Española in Spain, rösti in Switzerland, and Irish soda bread in Ireland. These Old World dishes were made in cast iron more than a hundred years ago, and cooks are still making them in cast iron today, with good reason. No other pan can achieve the same end results as cast iron.

It's time to rediscover the cast iron skillet. Whether yours once belonged to your grandmother or is a new preseasoned pan fresh out of the box, use it and enjoy it; it will only get better with time. Best of all, you'll find that it will bring generations together to cook, share good food, and create lasting memories.

YOUR CAST IRON PAN

Cast iron cookware has been around for hundreds of years. Centuries ago, cast iron kettles and skillets were used over open fires in Europe. They were one of the very few treasured items that settlers brought with them to the New World.

Cast iron pans are formed through the process of sand-casting. Molten iron is poured into a sand-clay mold of the desired shape. After it cools, the mold is removed and the pan's surface is smoothed by a stone-washing process. Although pioneer cast iron companies Griswold Manufacturing and Wagner Manufacturing are no longer in business, you can occasionally discover them at second-hand stores. They are a great find. Well-seasoned and well-used, they are our favorites. Lodge Manufacturing, founded in 1896, is the largest domestic producer of high-quality iron cookware. Lodge products are readily available in cookware shops and hardware stores throughout the country.

Today's cast iron pans come in a wide variety of shapes and sizes to suit almost any culinary need. We recommend pans from Lodge that are made in the United States. Their pieces range from skillets, Dutch ovens, grill pans, and griddles to specialty pans for breads, casseroles, and muffins. French-made Le Creuset's enamel-coated cast iron cookware, which is more expensive than traditional cast iron, is our favorite for soups and casseroles. Staub cast iron, also made in France, produces unique cast iron pieces sold in many different shapes and sizes. Both Le Creuset and Staub are available at specialty cookware stores such as Sur La Table. (See Resources, page 158.)

Often, cooks who are unfamiliar with cast iron are pleasantly surprised to find that well-seasoned cast iron has a perfect nonstick surface. Teflon-coated and stainless steel pans tend to cause food to "sweat," which stews and toughens meat instead of browning it, and prevents a crisp crust from forming. Food cooked in cast iron doesn't sweat. Cast iron pans heat quickly and evenly and maintain their heat. They provide an even exchange of heat with the food, thus allowing meats to brown and caramelize, staying tender. The high heat of the pan forms golden crusts on baked goods and acts just like a wood-fired oven for pizzas and breads.

Cast iron's versatility is what appeals to us the most. We use our cast iron skillets for pan-searing, pan-roasting, stir-frying, and baking. We find that an iron skillet is an excellent alternative to a wok—especially for those who cook on an electric stove. For camping, cast iron pans are indispensable. A Dutch oven is perfect for cooking over an outdoor fire, and it can be used either as an oven or as a slow cooker.

Purchasing Cast Iron Cookware

Today, most new pans come preseasoned, which means you can use them right out of the box. Even a preseasoned pan, however, will need to be reseasoned now and then to maintain its nonstick surface. Unseasoned new pans are gunmetal gray in color, but with proper care and much use they will develop the familiar black patina that is the hallmark of a well-seasoned skillet.

You have a lot of choices when shopping for a new cast iron pan. Keep in mind that you don't need every shape and size. We own 8-, 10- and 12-inch skillets—two with straight 2-inch sides for searing and roasting, and one with 4-inch sides for stewing and braising. We love our griddle pan for pancakes, bacon, and eggs cooked side by side. A grill pan is our indoor barbecue, perfect for grilling meats of all kinds.

Here are descriptions of our favorite skillets and pans. Note that most cast iron skillets do not come with lids. When we are in need of a lid, we use one from our cupboards that is the same size as the pan.

Skillets are generally straight sided and long handled, with sizes ranging from 6½ inches in diameter and 1¼ inches deep to 15¼ inches in diameter and 2¼ inches deep. (Sizes are indicated on the bottom of the skillet.) Large skillets have loop handles on either side, which make them easier to manage.

Lodge also has a stir-fry skillet, which resembles a wok and is 12¾ inches in diameter and 3¼ inches deep. If you like wok cookery, you'll find that this cast iron version works well on both electric and gas ranges.

Grill pans, both round and square, have raised ridges in the bottom of the pan, which make them ideal for cooking boneless, skinless chicken breasts, fish fillets, and steaks indoors. These pans are a wonderful alternative to an outdoor grill. Sizes range from 9 inches in diameter to roughly 11 inches in diameter; they are approximately 2 inches deep.

Dutch ovens have loop handles and always come with lids. They are approximately 4 to 5 inches deep and range in capacity from 5 quarts to 9 quarts. Note that Dutch ovens differ from "camp ovens" or "spiders." Camp ovens are deep like Dutch ovens but have three legs for setting on an open fire. (Dutch ovens have flat bottoms.) We have become reacquainted with our Dutch oven, and we use it indoors as well as outdoors. Lodge makes a great preseasoned, 6-quart Dutch oven perfect for stews and soups.

Griddles are flat with smooth surfaces. Some have grill ridges on one side. Our favorite is rectangular in shape and fits over two burners.

You will also find specialty cast iron pans used for specific recipes. The specialty pans we own are a popover pan, an ebelskiver pan, and a Swedish pancake pan. Season specialty cookware as you would any other cast iron pan, and always use a little butter or vegetable oil before adding batters.

Seasoning New Cast Iron and Reseasoning Old

The secret to successful cooking in cast iron is proper seasoning and care for your pans. The point of seasoning is to bake the fat into the pan's porous surface to create a smooth, permanent non-stick coating and to prevent rust.

If your new pan is not preseasoned, it will be coated with a thin layer of wax to prevent it from rusting. It's important to remove this before seasoning.

Place the pan in the sink and fill it with boiling water. Allow it to cool slightly, and then scrub well with a mild detergent and plastic scouring pad. If there's a lid, scrub that also. Then follow these steps for seasoning a new unseasoned pan or reseasoning an old pan:

1. Dry the pan thoroughly and coat it lightly with Crisco shortening, inside and out. (We don't recommend using vegetable or other liquid oils, as they can leave the pan sticky.)

2. Place the pan upside down on a baking sheet on a rack in the middle of the oven. Bake for one hour at 350°F. The pan will smoke, but the smoke will disappear after 20 minutes. Be sure to have your oven fan on. You can also do this on a baking sheet on your barbecue, with the lid closed.

3. Turn off the heat and let the pan cool completely in the oven.

The first few times you use a newly seasoned pan, it's best to fry bacon or other fatty foods. After these first uses you'll find that your pan will develop a permanent nonstick surface.

Caring for Cast Iron

Never wash a skillet in a dishwasher! Sometimes, especially after cooking egg dishes, you will have to briefly soak the skillet before scrubbing. Never use metal to scrape the pan. To clean and care for skillet after each use:

1. Hold the pan under hot water, add a little mild dishwashing soap, and scrub it clean with a nylon scrub pad or a stiff-bristled, nonmetal brush.

2. Dry the pan immediately with a towel and rub it lightly with olive oil to keep it from drying out.

3. Line the pan with a paper towel and store in a warm, dry place. Store lids separately to allow air to circulate around the pan and lid to prevent condensation, which can lead to rust spots; or keep your pan in the oven, and every time you turn it on the pan will reseason itself.

4. If food begins to stick, simply place the pan on the burner on high heat for a minute or two. Take the pan off the heat source and sprinkle in a half-teaspoon of salt and a teaspoon of olive oil. Using an old rag, scrub the inside of the pan. Wipe out any leftover salt and let the pan cool. After

the pan has cooled, buff it one more time with a clean rag. That's all there is to it!

If you find a rusted cast iron pan at an antique shop or garage sale, you *can* rescue it. Simply scour the pan with a plastic scouring pad, and then wash in hot, soapy water. Rinse well and dry thoroughly with a towel or on a burner over low heat. Then follow the seasoning instructions above. If you find a pan that is crusted with grease, put it in a large pot of boiling water with 1 cup of baking soda and boil for 10 minutes, then scrub with a scouring pad and reseason your pan.

Cooking with Cast Iron

Cast iron heats very evenly, so you don't need to cook at high temperatures. Most of the time we use medium heat.

Remember that the handles of cast iron pans heat up, so keep oven mitts close by when using a skillet. We use heat-resistant handle covers designed for cast iron skillets. Because the pans are heavy, always use two hands (and two oven mitts!) when lifting a hot skillet. Cast iron stays hot long after it has been removed from the heat, so remember to use a trivet when placing your pan on a table or countertop.

When you are ready to cook, heat your skillet over medium heat before adding food to the pan. To test the heat, sprinkle in a few drops of water; the droplets will dance across the pan.

Don't store food in a cast iron skillet because the pan will impart a metallic taste. Always remove food and wash the pan immediately after cooking.

Cast iron pans do demand a bit of care, but once you've cooked in one, we're certain you will agree that they are well worth the effort.

BREAKFAST & BRUNCH

Classic Buttermilk Pancakes
Tortilla Española
Dutch Baby
Savory Dutch Baby
Amazing Popovers
Swedish Pancakes
Ebelskivers
Overnight French Toast
Dungeness Crab and Tillamook Cheddar Soufflé
Zucchini-Onion Frittata
Joe's Special
Beef Brisket Hash with Yukon Gold Potatoes
Buttermilk Breakfast Scones with Dried Currants
Mom's Amazing Banana Bread
Grandmother Kramis's Irish Soda Bread
Brown Sugar Coffee Cake
Pecan Sticky Buns

1

If you have fond memories connected to a cast iron skillet, they probably have something to do with breakfast. The smells of sausage and eggs cooking in a cast iron skillet are a wonderful greeting in the morning.

We can't say it enough: So many foods are at their best when cooked in cast iron. Because cast iron conducts heat so evenly, bacon gets crisp and pancakes come out golden brown. Coffee cakes are golden on the outside, incredibly moist on the inside.

Take a few minutes on Saturday afternoon to prepare Overnight French Toast. Sunday morning, your family can enjoy making breakfast together. Other recipes can easily be made during your first cup of coffee. Our family likes to use the big cast iron griddle to cook pancakes and sausages side by side.

So make some coffee, pour the fresh-squeezed orange juice, heat up your griddle, and enjoy a leisurely breakfast with your family.

CLASSIC BUTTERMILK PANCAKES

Saturday morning is pancake time. Weekdays are so busy; it's fun to relax and enjoy a leisurely breakfast when the weekend rolls around. The cast iron skillet or griddle cooks perfect pancakes every time. In the summer, sprinkle fresh blueberries or huckleberries on top of the pancakes while they are cooking, before you turn them over.

• • • • •

MAKES 24 FOUR-INCH PANCAKES

2 cups all-purpose flour
2 tablespoons sugar
2 teaspoons baking powder
½ teaspoon salt
2 eggs
2 cups buttermilk
½ cup whole milk
¼ cup (½ stick) salted butter, melted, plus additional melted butter
   for serving
1 tablespoon vegetable oil, plus more if needed

• • • • •

Warm maple syrup, for serving

⬤ In a large bowl, combine the flour, sugar, baking powder, and salt. In another bowl, whisk the eggs, buttermilk, milk, and melted butter until well blended. Add the egg mixture to the flour mixture and whisk just until combined.

⬤ Heat a 10- or 12-inch cast iron skillet or a cast iron griddle over medium heat. Add 1 tablespoon vegetable oil to the skillet. Pour the batter into the skillet, ¼ cup at a time, forming small pancakes. When bubbles start to form, turn the pancakes over and cook until golden brown, 2 to 3 minutes longer. Continue until all the batter is used up, adding more vegetable oil as necessary. Serve with melted butter and warm maple syrup.

TORTILLA ESPAÑOLA
(Spanish Potato Omelet)

Similar to a frittata, this traditional Spanish dish can be served warm or cold. A friend of ours once brought it on a ski trip, and we sat in the sun enjoying this delicious potato omelet. The dish turns out golden brown and moist, with layers of potato.

• • ● • •

MAKES 4 SERVINGS

¼ cup extra virgin olive oil, plus 2 tablespoons
1 medium yellow onion, cut into ¼-inch-thick slices
    (about 1 cup)
1 pound Yukon Gold or red-skinned potatoes, peeled, halved, and cut
    into ¼-inch slices
Salt and freshly ground black pepper
6 eggs

• • • • •

Sour cream, for serving
Hot sauce, for serving

● Place a 10-inch cast iron skillet over medium heat. Add 2 tablespoons olive oil and onions and cook, stirring occasionally, for about 5 minutes. Turn down the heat to medium low and cook until golden brown, about 15 minutes. Remove to a large bowl and set aside.

● Heat the skillet over medium heat, then add ¼ cup olive oil and allow oil to heat up, about 2 minutes. Carefully add potatoes and cook about 10 minutes (reduce the heat if smoking occurs). Carefully separate the potato slices to keep them from sticking together. Remove the potatoes with a slotted spoon to a baking sheet lined with paper towels to absorb the excess oil. Sprinkle with salt and pepper. Set skillet aside, reserving the remaining olive oil inside.

● Break the eggs into a medium bowl and season with salt and pepper. Whisk until frothy. Add the cooked potatoes and onions to the eggs.

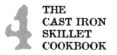

- Position a rack at the top of the oven and preheat the broiler.

- Place the skillet with the remaining olive oil over medium heat. When the pan is hot pour the egg mixture into the skillet and quickly reduce the heat to low. Cook until the pan side of the omelet is golden brown, about 5 minutes. Place the skillet in the oven and broil until the top of the omelet is golden brown, about 3 to 5 minutes more.

- Season with salt and freshly ground pepper. Use a spatula to loosen the omelet from the pan, and slide the omelet onto a warmed plate. Cut into wedges and serve with sour cream and your favorite hot sauce.

DUTCH BABY

This is a recipe meant for the cast iron skillet. Just a few ingredients produce an amazing puffed pancake that looks as though it might rise right out of the pan. We like to serve this puffed pancake on lazy Saturday mornings and, even more, we love getting it served to us on Mother's Day.

• • • • •

MAKES 2 SERVINGS

2 tablespoons butter
4 extra-large eggs
½ cup all-purpose flour
½ cup milk

Topping
3 tablespoons butter
Juice of 1 lemon
½ cup powdered sugar

● Preheat the oven to 425°F. To make the Dutch baby, melt the butter in a 12-inch cast iron skillet over low heat. Mix the eggs, flour, and milk in a blender on medium speed until just blended, 5 to 10 seconds. Pour the batter into the skillet with the melted butter.

● Place the skillet in the oven and bake until the top puffs up and is lightly golden, about 25 minutes.

● To clarify the butter for the topping, melt it over low heat in a small saucepan. Skim off and discard the foam. Remove from the heat and let stand until the solids settle, about 5 minutes. Pour through a strainer into a glass measuring cup.

● When the Dutch baby is done, drizzle the clarified butter over the top, then sprinkle with the lemon juice and dust with the powdered sugar. Cut into six wedges and serve immediately.

SAVORY DUTCH BABY

This recipe adds ham and cheese to the traditional Dutch baby, making a heartier variation suitable for lunch or dinner.

• • ● • •

MAKES 2 SERVINGS

3 tablespoons butter
4 extra-large eggs
½ cup all-purpose flour
½ cup whole milk
½ cup grated Swiss or Gruyère cheese
½ cup (about three ¼-inch-thick slices) chopped ham (French, Black Forest, or honey)

● Preheat the oven to 425°F. To make the Dutch baby, melt the butter in a 12-inch cast iron skillet over low heat. Mix the eggs, flour, and milk in a blender on medium speed until just blended, 5 to 10 seconds. Pour the batter into a medium bowl and add the cheese and ham, folding them into the mixture. Pour into the skillet with the melted butter.

● Place the skillet in the oven and bake until the top puffs up and is lightly golden, 20 to 25 minutes.

● When the Dutch baby is done, cut into six wedges and serve immediately.

AMAZING POPOVERS

Serve these hot out of the oven with butter and strawberry jam. The cast iron popover pan cooks evenly and results in crisp, golden breakfast treats.

• • ● • •

MAKES 6 SERVINGS

1 cup all-purpose flour
½ teaspoon salt
1 cup milk, heated to 90°F to 100°F
2 large eggs, at room temperature
1 tablespoon butter, melted
1 tablespoon vegetable oil

● Preheat oven to 375°F.

● In a medium-sized bowl combine flour and salt. In another medium-sized bowl, mix milk and eggs with a whisk and stir in butter. Gradually whisk in the flour and salt with a pastry brush. Coat the inside of the popover cups with the vegetable oil.

● Place the popover pan in the preheated oven for 5 minutes. Then remove from the oven and fill each popover cup with ½ cup of the batter. Return to the oven and bake for 35 to 40 minutes, until puffed and golden.

SWEDISH PANCAKES

Light and delicious, these pancakes are not heavy "sinkers." This is another traditional recipe from our Northwest Scandinavian community. We use a Swedish pancake pan with six shallow circles that shape the pancakes perfectly, but you can use your skillet or griddle.

• • • • •

MAKES 4 SERVINGS

3 extra-large eggs, separated
2 cups whole milk
⅛ teaspoon salt
1 cup all-purpose flour
2 tablespoons butter, melted, plus additional melted butter for serving

• • • • •

Fresh berry syrup, for serving

● In a large bowl, beat the egg yolks, milk, salt, flour, and 2 tablespoons melted butter. Using an electric mixer, beat the egg whites until soft peaks form, then fold them into the batter.

● Heat a cast iron skillet or griddle over medium heat. Drop about ¼ cup of batter into the hot skillet for each pancake. They should be small, 2 to 3 inches across. Cook until golden brown on both sides. Serve with melted butter and fresh berry syrup.

EBELSKIVERS
(Scandinavian Pancakes)

Ebelskivers are like little doughnuts without the fat. This recipe calls for a special cast iron pan, with seven round molds. You drop some of the batter into each mold, cook for 2 minutes, turn and cook on the other side, and you have these amazing, golden Scandinavian treats. Ebelskivers are also delicious cut in half and served with mascarpone and fresh berry jam.

• • ● • •

MAKES 4 TO 6 SERVINGS

1½ cups all-purpose flour
1 teaspoon baking powder
½ teaspoon baking soda
¼ teaspoon salt
2 eggs, beaten
2 cups sour cream
½ cup milk
3½ teaspoons butter, divided

• • ● • •

Jam or maple syrup and powdered sugar, for serving

● Sift the flour, baking powder, baking soda, and salt into a large bowl. In a small bowl, whisk together the eggs, sour cream, and milk. Add the egg mixture to the flour mixture and beat by hand or with an electric mixer until smooth.

● Heat a cast iron ebelskiver pan over medium-low heat. Place ½ teaspoon butter in each indentation, allow to melt, and then fill each halfway with batter. Cook until light brown, about 2 minutes. Turn gently with a fork and brown the other side. Transfer to a platter and serve with maple syrup and powdered sugar.

OVERNIGHT FRENCH TOAST

The cast iron skillet browns and crisps French toast better than any other pan. Soaking the bread the night before makes the final result light and fluffy. Crispy browned link sausages make a good accompaniment.

• • • • •

MAKES 4 SERVINGS

1 baguette, cut into 1-inch-thick slices
1½ cups half-and-half
4 eggs
¼ cup sugar
⅛ teaspoon salt
1 teaspoon vanilla extract
2 tablespoons butter, plus more as needed
1 tablespoon vegetable oil, plus more as needed

• • • • •

Warm maple syrup, for serving

● Place the baguette slices in a 9- x 13-inch pan. In a medium bowl, whisk together the half-and-half, eggs, sugar, salt, and vanilla. Pour over the bread slices, turning the slices to coat well. Cover with plastic wrap and refrigerate overnight. (If your time is limited, 1 hour ahead works just fine.)

● Position a rack in the center of the oven, and preheat to 350°F.

● Melt 2 tablespoons butter in a 10- or 12-inch cast iron skillet or a cast iron griddle over medium heat. Add 1 tablespoon vegetable oil. Just after the butter foams, add 6 slices of the bread and cook for 2 minutes. Turn and cook for 2 minutes longer. After the second side is golden brown, transfer to a baking sheet in the oven for 10 minutes to finish cooking. Repeat with the remaining slices of bread, adding more butter and oil to the skillet as needed for cooking. Serve on warm plates with warm maple syrup.

DUNGENESS CRAB AND TILLAMOOK CHEDDAR SOUFFLÉ

The combination of bread, eggs, cream, and overnight soaking results in a soufflé-like dish. Assemble this dish the night before and then bake it in the morning. Instead of using crab, you can cook 1 pound of breakfast sausages and then cut each one into thirds and mix with the bread and cheese.

• • ● • •

MAKES 8 SERVINGS

6 large eggs
2 cups half-and-half
2 cups grated Tillamook cheddar cheese
10 slices French bread, cut into 1-inch cubes
8 ounces Dungeness crabmeat

• • ● • •

2 tablespoons chopped fresh parsley
Fresh tomato salsa, for serving

● Generously butter a 10-inch cast iron skillet. Whisk the eggs and half-and-half together in a medium bowl until well blended. In another bowl, mix together the cheese, bread cubes, and crab, then spread this mixture evenly in the buttered skillet. Pour the egg mixture over the top. Cover and refrigerate for at least 2 hours or overnight.

● When ready to bake, position a rack in the center of the oven and preheat to 350°F. Place the skillet in the oven and bake until puffed and lightly browned, about 50 minutes. Remove from the oven, sprinkle with parsley, cut into wedges, and serve with a fresh tomato salsa.

ZUCCHINI-ONION FRITTATA

Not just for the breakfast menu, this egg dish, which is served at room tempera-
ture, is a perfect accompaniment to roast chicken for picnics. The skillet cooks
the frittata low and slow and forms a delicious crust.

• • • • •

MAKES 8 SERVINGS

6 tablespoons extra-virgin olive oil
1 sweet yellow onion, quartered and thinly sliced into
   ¼-inch crescents
2 teaspoons dried Italian herb seasoning
9 small zucchini (2 pounds), washed, dried, halved lengthwise, and
   cut into ¼-inch-thick slices
1 teaspoon sea salt
Freshly ground black pepper
¼ cup fresh bread crumbs
1½ cups finely grated Parmesan cheese, divided
9 large eggs

• • • • •

Salsa and sour cream, for serving

● Position a rack in the center of the oven and preheat to 300°F.

● Warm 4 tablespoons of the olive oil in a 10-inch cast iron skillet over
medium heat. Add the onions, stirring to coat with the olive oil. Sprinkle
the herb seasoning over the onions and cook for 5 minutes. Add the zucchini and stir gently to mix with the onions. Reduce the heat to low, cover,
and cook until the zucchini softens, about 8 minutes.

● Remove from the heat and drain off any liquid from the pan. Spread
the onions and zucchini evenly in the skillet. Season with salt and pepper.
Sprinkle with the bread crumbs and 1 cup of the Parmesan cheese.

● Crack the eggs into a medium bowl and whisk until well blended. Pour
over the zucchini mixture, cover the pan loosely with foil, and bake for 45
minutes.

recipe continues next page

● Remove the foil and sprinkle with the remaining ½ cup cheese. Raise the oven rack 3 inches. Preheat the broiler and broil until the frittata is golden brown on top, 2 to 3 minutes. Drizzle the remaining 2 tablespoons of olive oil over the frittata. Slice into wedges and serve with salsa and sour cream.

● If not serving right away, remove the wedges from the skillet, using a slotted spatula to drain off extra juices. Transfer to a serving platter and keep warm.

JOE'S SPECIAL

This San Francisco specialty is a quick, easy egg dish. It might look messy, but it is delicious to eat. Serve with Tabasco sauce and crisp buttered toast. The skillet browns the meat and cooks the eggs. To clean the skillet after you're finished, soak the pan briefly, and then scour lightly with a plastic scrubbing pad.

• • • • •

MAKES 4 SERVINGS

2 tablespoons butter

1 cup chopped yellow onion (about ½ onion)

1 tablespoon chopped fresh oregano, or 1 teaspoon dried oregano

12 ounces lean ground beef

½ teaspoon freshly ground black pepper

3 ounces baby spinach, coarsely chopped

6 eggs, beaten

½ cup grated Parmesan cheese, plus more for garnish

¼ cup chopped red bell pepper (about ¼ pepper), plus more for garnish

• • • • •

Toast, for serving

❋ Melt the butter in a 10-inch cast iron skillet over medium heat. Add the onions and cook, stirring occasionally, until soft, 3 to 4 minutes. Sprinkle the oregano over the onions. Crumble the ground beef into the pan. Cook, stirring often, until the beef is evenly browned, 3 to 5 minutes. Add the black pepper and spinach. Cook and stir until the spinach wilts. Add the beaten eggs and stir everything together. Add the Parmesan cheese and bell pepper. Continue stirring until the eggs are cooked. Serve on warm plates with freshly made toast. Sprinkle additional cheese and chopped bell pepper over each serving.

BEEF BRISKET HASH
WITH YUKON GOLD POTATOES

We love to use the cast iron skillet for this dish because we can achieve a nice golden crust. The crust scrapes away from the pan and adds flavor to the hash. Make the Slow-Roasted Beef Brisket (see page 54) on Sunday, and then on Monday evening use the leftover beef brisket to make this easy and delicious hash.

• • • • •

MAKES 4 SERVINGS

¼ cup (½ stick) salted butter
1 cup diced yellow onion (about ½ onion)
6 cups peeled, diced, and cooked Yukon Gold potatoes (about 2 pounds)
4 cups chopped leftover beef brisket
½ cup heavy cream
Salt and lots of freshly ground black pepper

• • • • •

3 tablespoons fresh chopped parsley, for garnish
Chili sauce or ketchup, for serving

● Melt the butter in a 10- or 12-inch cast iron skillet over medium heat. Add the onions and cook for 5 minutes. Stir in the potatoes and meat and cook for 10 minutes. Add the cream and stir gently. Be sure to scrape up the crispy crust that forms on the bottom of the pan. Cook until hot and the potatoes are nicely browned. Season to taste with salt and pepper. Sprinkle with chopped parsley. Serve with chili sauce or ketchup.

BUTTERMILK BREAKFAST SCONES WITH DRIED CURRANTS

These traditional flaky scones are delicious split in half and topped with sweet butter and fresh raspberry jam.

• • ● • •

MAKES 12 SCONES

Scones
3 cups unbleached all-purpose flour
1/3 cup sugar
2 1/2 teaspoons baking powder
1/2 teaspoon baking soda
3/4 teaspoon salt
3/4 cup (1 1/2 sticks) chilled butter, cut into 6 to 8 pieces
1/2 cup dried currants
1 teaspoon grated orange zest
1 cup buttermilk

Glaze
1 tablespoon heavy cream
1/4 teaspoon ground cinnamon
2 tablespoons sugar

● Position a rack in the center of the oven and preheat to 400°F.

● To prepare the scones, stir the flour, sugar, baking powder, baking soda, and salt together in a large bowl. Add the butter and beat with an electric mixer just until blended. Add the currants and orange zest. Pour in the buttermilk and mix just until blended.

● Gather the dough into a ball. On a lightly floured board, roll the dough out into a circle, approximately 1/2 to 3/4 inch thick. Cut the circle into 12 wedges.

● Place the scones in a circle, 1/2 inch apart, in a well-buttered 12-inch cast iron skillet, and bake until golden, about 20 to 25 minutes. Remove from the oven.

● While the scones are baking, prepare the glaze, combining the cream, cinnamon, and sugar in a small bowl. After removing the scones from the oven, brush with the glaze and serve.

MOM'S AMAZING BANANA BREAD

The cardamom gives this banana bread a surprisingly nice flavor. The skillet makes the outside of the bread golden and crisp, while the bananas and sour cream keep the inside moist. We love to toast our banana bread and spread cream cheese over the top.

• • ● • •

MAKES 8 SERVINGS

½ cup (1 stick) unsalted butter, at room temperature
½ cup granulated sugar
½ cup light brown sugar
2 eggs
3 overripe bananas, well mashed
½ teaspoon vanilla extract
2 cups all-purpose flour
1 teaspoon baking soda
¼ teaspoon salt
½ teaspoon ground cinnamon
½ teaspoon ground cardamom
Dash ground allspice
¼ cup chopped pecans or walnuts
¼ cup sour cream

● Preheat the oven to 350°F. Using an electric mixer on medium-high speed, beat the butter, granulated sugar, and brown sugar in a large bowl until smooth and creamy. Beat in the eggs, one at a time, then beat in the bananas and vanilla.

● In a separate bowl, mix together the flour, baking soda, salt, cinnamon, cardamom, and allspice. Add the flour mixture to the banana mixture and fold in with a spatula until well blended. Gently fold the nuts and sour cream into the batter until just blended, being careful not to overmix.

Lightly butter a 10- or 12-inch cast iron skillet. Pour the batter into the skillet; place in the oven and bake until a toothpick inserted in the center comes out clean, 45 minutes to 1 hour.

Remove from the oven and let cool in the pan. To serve, you can either flip the bread out of the pan or serve it in the skillet, sliced into wedges.

GRANDMOTHER KRAMIS'S IRISH SODA BREAD

The cast iron skillet works wonders for Irish Soda Bread. That's how our Irish grandmother made it, and that's how we've always done it, too. We break a wedge in half and spread it with the Whipped Orange Butter before settling down with a cup of hot tea.

• • ● • •

MAKES 8 SERVINGS

4 cups all-purpose flour
1 teaspoon baking soda
2 teaspoons baking powder
½ cup sugar
½ cup currants, or 1 cup raisins
Pinch salt
½ cup (1 stick) unsalted butter, melted
2 eggs
2 cups buttermilk

• • ● • •

Whipped Orange Butter, for serving (see note)

● Position a rack in the center of the oven and preheat to 350°F.

● In a large bowl, mix together the flour, baking soda, baking powder, sugar, currants, and salt. In a small bowl, whisk together the butter, eggs, and buttermilk. Pour the butter mixture into the flour mixture and stir with a spoon until it forms a dough. Place the dough onto a lightly floured surface and knead until well combined. Butter a 10-inch cast iron skillet and place the dough in the skillet, flattening it to fill the bottom of the pan. Score a large X across the top of the dough. Bake until a toothpick inserted in the center of the bread comes out clean, 25 to 30 minutes.

Note: **To make the Whipped Orange Butter, whip softened butter with a whisk until it is light and fluffy. Whisk in grated orange zest to taste and spread on soda bread.**

BROWN SUGAR COFFEE CAKE

Nothing looks better on a Sunday morning than a warm coffee cake, still in the skillet, in the center of the kitchen table. The sour cream makes it moist, contrasting perfectly with the crisp walnuts, cinnamon, and brown sugar on top.

• • • • •

MAKES 12 SERVINGS

Cake
1 cup (2 sticks) salted butter, at room temperature, cut into 8 pieces
1 cup light brown sugar
2 large eggs
1 teaspoon vanilla extract
3/4 cup sour cream
2 1/2 cups all-purpose flour
1 1/2 teaspoons baking powder

Topping
1/2 cup all-purpose flour
3/4 cup light brown sugar
1 teaspoon ground cinnamon
6 tablespoons (3/4 stick) chilled butter, cut into 4 pieces
1 cup chopped walnuts

Position a rack in the center of the oven and preheat to 350°F.

To prepare the cake, place the butter in a large mixing bowl. Add the brown sugar and beat with an electric mixer until light and fluffy. Add the eggs, one at a time, beating after each addition. With a rubber spatula, blend in the vanilla and sour cream. In a separate bowl, mix together the flour and baking powder, then fold into the butter mixture until completely blended. Generously butter a 12-inch cast iron skillet. Spread the batter evenly in the skillet.

To prepare the topping, mix together the flour, brown sugar, cinnamon, and chilled butter with your fingers until evenly blended. Sprinkle evenly over the cake batter. Sprinkle the walnuts over the top. Place the skillet in the oven and bake for 35 to 40 minutes. When you gently touch the center of the cake with your fingers, it should feel firm to your touch. Serve warm.

PECAN STICKY BUNS

The cast iron skillet heats so evenly that these rolls come out golden brown, with an amazing caramel sauce on the bottom.

• • ● • •

MAKES 12 ROLLS

Dough
1 package dry yeast
¼ cup warm water
½ cup cake flour
⅓ cup granulated sugar
1 teaspoon salt
1 teaspoon vanilla extract
¼ cup milk
2 eggs
2 cups all-purpose flour
6 tablespoons (¾ stick) unsalted butter, at room temperature

Glaze
⅔ cup light brown sugar
6 tablespoons (¾ stick) unsalted butter, at room temperature
3 tablespoons honey
3 tablespoons dark corn syrup
3 tablespoons water
1 cup pecan halves, coarsely chopped

Filling
2 teaspoons ground cinnamon
¼ teaspoon freshly grated nutmeg
½ cup granulated sugar
2 cups raisins, softened in hot water and drained (optional)
¼ cup (½ stick) unsalted butter, softened

To prepare the dough, dissolve the yeast in the warm water in a mixing bowl. Let rest for 5 minutes. Add the cake flour, granulated sugar, salt, vanilla, milk, and eggs. In a mixing bowl with dough hook attachment, mix on low speed or by hand until blended. Slowly add the all-purpose flour and mix well. Add the butter and knead or mix with dough hook until butter is incorporated and dough is smooth. Place in a well-greased bowl, cover with plastic wrap, and let rise until doubled in size, about 45 minutes. Punch down dough, knead a couple times, cover, and allow to double again in a warm place for 4 hours.

While the dough rises, prepare the glaze. Place the brown sugar, butter, honey, corn syrup, and water in an 8- or 10-inch cast iron skillet and mix well. Place the skillet over medium heat and cook, without stirring, until the butter is melted and the liquid is bubbling, about 5 minutes. Sprinkle the pecans evenly over the glaze, remove from the heat, and let cool.

Remove dough from bowl and transfer to a lightly floured surface. Roll the dough into a 10- by 15-inch rectangle. To prepare the filling, mix together the cinnamon, nutmeg, granulated sugar, and raisins (if using). Spread the softened butter over the dough, and sprinkle the dough with the sugar-raisin mixture. Roll up like a jelly roll (starting from the 15-inch side), then cut into 1½-inch slices by sliding a thread under the roll, crossing the ends over the top, and pulling tight. (This way the dough isn't compressed.) Place the slices flat on top of the glaze in the skillet and let them rise for 30 minutes.

While the buns are rising, position a rack in the center of the oven and preheat to 375°F.

Bake the buns for 20 to 25 minutes, until golden brown and firm to the touch. Protecting both hands with oven mitts, grasp the skillet and carefully turn sticky buns onto a slightly larger plate. Serve warm.

APPETIZERS

Grilled Prosciutto-Wrapped Radicchio with Balsamic Vinegar and Olive Oil
Queso Fundido Verde
Asian Beef with Lettuce Wraps and Sweet Chili Sauce
Pan-Roasted Wild Mushroom Crostini and Chèvre
Crispy Lamb Skewers
Golden Fried Oysters
Dungeness Crab Quesadillas with Avocado-Lime Sauce
Garlic Spiced Prawns
Eggplant-Pepper Tapenade

These recipes for appetizers offer a melting pot of flavors from around the world. Queso Fundido Verde, served hot and bubbling in the skillet, is a warm centerpiece that everyone likes to gather around. The Eggplant-Pepper Tapenade brings a taste of the Mediterranean to your table and is a perfect dish to serve with other appetizers. We love the sweet and spicy flavors of the Asian Beef, and the lettuce wraps are a fun presentation. Quesadillas are a good example of how you can use your cast iron skillet to quickly create an afternoon snack or a predinner appetizer. Although these appetizers are made to order, you can have them ready ahead of time and then cook them and serve them hot to your guests.

GRILLED PROSCIUTTO-WRAPPED RADICCHIO WITH BALSAMIC VINEGAR AND OLIVE OIL

The radicchio's bitterness, the prosciutto's saltiness, and the balsamic vinegar's tart sweetness perform the perfect balancing act, resulting in a flavor combination that practically explodes in your mouth.

• • ● • •

MAKES 8 SERVINGS

> 2 small heads radicchio, cut into eighths
> 8 to 10 slices prosciutto, sliced in half lengthwise
> 4 tablespoons extra virgin olive oil, divided
> ¼ cup balsamic vinegar
> Freshly ground black pepper

● Wrap each piece of radicchio tightly with a slice of prosciutto.

● Divide the radicchio into two batches. Heat 2 tablespoons of the olive oil in a 10- or 12-inch cast iron skillet over medium-high heat. Place the first batch of wrapped radicchio in the pan and sear on all sides until the prosciutto browns and the radicchio starts to soften and changes to a deeper burgundy color, about 5 minutes. Transfer to a plate. Repeat with the remaining olive oil and the second batch of wrapped radicchio.

● Drizzle the radicchio with the balsamic vinegar and season with freshly ground black pepper. Serve immediately.

QUESO FUNDIDO VERDE

Seattle's Cactus restaurant is one of our favorites because they use great ingredients and combine amazing flavors. They shared their recipe for Queso Fundido Verde with us because it works so well in an iron skillet. This dish turns out like a Mexican version of fondue, with chorizo sausage crumbled over the top. You can also heat and serve this dish in four 4-inch skillets: Just place 1 cup of the fundido mixture into each skillet and broil for 3 to 5 minutes. Serve with tortilla chips and, of course, margaritas!

• • ● • •

MAKES 4 SERVINGS

2 poblano chiles
8 ounces chorizo sausage
2½ cups (20 ounces) cream cheese, at room temperature
1 cup mayonnaise
½ cup finely chopped green onion, plus additional for garnish
½ cup chopped white onion
2 teaspoons minced garlic
2⅔ cups grated Jack cheese
1 cup crumbled feta cheese
¾ cup fresh or frozen corn, thawed and drained if frozen
½ cup diced red bell pepper

• • ● • •

1 lime, quartered, for garnish
Tortilla chips, for serving

● To roast the poblano chiles, place them directly over the flame of a gas stove or in a cast iron skillet over medium-high heat. Roast, turning occasionally, until the skin blackens, about 10 minutes. Transfer to a paper bag for 10 minutes to loosen the skin and cool the chiles. Remove from the bag and wipe with a damp paper towel to remove the skin. Make a cut in each chile to release the steam, then halve them, remove the stem and seeds, and dice into ⅜-inch pieces.

● To prepare the chorizo, push the meat out of the casing. Heat a cast iron skillet over medium heat. Add the chorizo, breaking the meat apart with a wooden spoon. Cook, stirring occasionally, until the fat cooks out of the sausage and the sausage turns golden brown, about 5 minutes. Transfer to a bowl using a slotted spoon, and set aside.

● Position a rack at the top of the oven and preheat to 400°F.

● To prepare the fundido, place the cream cheese in a large bowl and mix with an electric mixer or by hand until smooth. Scrape down the sides of the bowl with a spatula. Add the mayonnaise and mix until smooth and free of lumps. Add the green onion, white onion, garlic, Jack cheese, feta, corn, bell pepper, and roasted poblano chiles to the cream cheese mixture. Mix until well combined.

● Place the cream cheese mixture in an 8-inch cast iron skillet. Bake for 10 minutes, until the edges are bubbling and the top is beginning to brown. Garnish with the chorizo, chopped green onions, and a lime wedge. Serve in the skillet with a big bowl of tortilla chips.

ASIAN BEEF WITH LETTUCE WRAPS AND SWEET CHILI SAUCE

The wonderful Slanted Door restaurant in San Francisco inspired this recipe. The sugars in the marinade caramelize beautifully when you brown the beef in an iron skillet, and the lettuce adds a fresh crunch. Set out the warm cooked beef, lettuce leaves, cilantro sprigs, and Sweet Chili Sauce, and let your guests assemble their own wrap.

• • • • •

MAKES 12 SERVINGS

Sweet Chili Sauce

1 tablespoon Thai sweet chili sauce
1 clove garlic, thinly sliced
¼ cup rice wine vinegar
1 serrano chile, thinly sliced
2 tablespoons fish sauce
2 tablespoons fresh lime juice
1 tablespoon unsalted peanuts, finely chopped (optional)

Vinaigrette

2 tablespoons canola oil
½ cup rice wine vinegar
2 tablespoons sugar
¼ cup soy sauce
2 tablespoons fish sauce

· · ● · ·

2 tablespoons sugar
2 tablespoons minced garlic (about 3 cloves)
Salt and freshly ground black pepper
1½ pounds top sirloin or filet mignon, trimmed and cut into ¾-inch
    cubes
1½ tablespoons butter, divided
Juice of ½ lime
12 medium Bibb lettuce leaves

· · ● · ·

Fresh cilantro sprigs, for serving

● Position a rack in the center of the oven and preheat to 250°F.

● To prepare the sauce, whisk together the chili sauce, garlic, rice wine vinegar, serrano chile, fish sauce, lime juice, and peanuts (if using) in a bowl. Set aside.

● To prepare the vinaigrette, whisk together the oil, rice wine vinegar, sugar, soy sauce, and fish sauce in a separate bowl. Set aside. Arrange the lettuce leaves on a large platter and refrigerate until needed.

● To prepare the beef, mix together the sugar, garlic, salt, and pepper in a large bowl. Add the beef and mix well to coat.

● Divide the beef into 3 batches for cooking (or else it will stew instead of brown). Place a 10- or 12-inch cast iron skillet over medium-high heat and melt ½ tablespoon of butter per batch of beef (do not crowd the pan). Add the first batch of beef, browning on both sides. Then add 2 tablespoons of the vinaigrette, turning quickly, until cooked to medium rare, about 3 minutes. Transfer the meat to a plate and keep it warm in the oven. Wipe out skillet and repeat with the other two batches of meat. After all the meat is browned, squeeze the fresh lime juice over the top.

● To assemble, place a few pieces of beef inside a lettuce leaf with a couple of cilantro sprigs, spoon over a little sauce, and roll up.

PAN-ROASTED WILD MUSHROOM CROSTINI AND CHÈVRE

In the Pacific Northwest, where we live, chanterelles come up after the first rain in September. You can make the crostini up to several days ahead and spoon on the warm mushroom topping when you are ready to serve.

• • • • •

MAKES 8 SERVINGS

Crostini
1 thin French baguette, cut into ½-inch-thick slices
½ cup extra virgin olive oil
2 tablespoons dried herbes de Provence

Mushroom Topping
1 pound chanterelle mushrooms, cleaned and air dried
1 teaspoon fresh thyme leaves
1 teaspoon chopped fresh rosemary
¼ cup extra virgin olive oil
1 tablespoon Worcestershire sauce
Salt and freshly ground black pepper
¼ cup finely chopped parsley
6 ounces chèvre

● Position a rack in the center of the oven and preheat to 375°F.

● To prepare the crostini, place the baguette slices on a baking sheet. Brush the top side of each slice with the olive oil. Sprinkle with the herbes de Provence and bake until crisp, 12 to 15 minutes. Remove from the oven and let cool on the baking sheet. When cool, store in sealed plastic bags until ready to use.

● To prepare the mushroom topping, preheat the oven to 450°F. Place a 10- or 12-inch cast iron skillet in the oven to preheat.

• Meanwhile, coarsely chop the mushrooms into ½-inch pieces. In a medium bowl, toss together the mushrooms, thyme, rosemary, and olive oil. Spread evenly in the preheated skillet and return to the oven. Roast for 12 to 15 minutes. Remove from the oven and drizzle the Worcestershire sauce over the mushrooms. Season to taste with salt and pepper, and sprinkle with the chopped parsley.

• To serve, spread each crostini with chèvre and top with warm mushrooms.

CRISPY LAMB SKEWERS

These tasty little lamb sausages get nice and crisp on the outside. Served hot, they are a great way to enjoy ground lamb. They don't taste gamy or greasy! Serve with tzatziki and hummus dips with pita wedges.

• • ● • •

MAKES 12 SKEWERS

1 pound ground lamb
½ teaspoon paprika
½ teaspoon ground cumin
1 teaspoon ground coriander
2 cloves garlic, minced
Salt and freshly ground black pepper
2 tablespoons finely chopped parsley (about 5 sprigs)
12 skewers
2 pitas

• • • • •

Tzatziki sauce, for serving
Hummus, for serving

● In a large bowl, mix together the lamb, paprika, cumin, coriander, and garlic. Season with salt and pepper. Using about 3 tablespoons of the mixture each time, form into small sausage shapes. You should have about 12 "sausages."

● Divide the sausages into two batches. Heat a 10- to 12-inch cast iron skillet over medium-high heat and cook the first batch, turning occasionally, until golden brown on all sides, 6 to 8 minutes. Transfer to a paper towel. Repeat with the second batch.

● Place the chopped parsley in a shallow dish, roll the lamb sausages in the parsley to coat, and skewer each sausage down the middle. Transfer to a serving dish.

● Wipe the skillet with a paper towel and place over medium heat. Warm each pita until light brown, and slice into 6 wedges. Spread tzatziki or hummus on the pita bread, and then place the lamb sausages inside or on top of the pitas.

GOLDEN FRIED OYSTERS

The plumpest oysters are available only in months that have an "R" in them. March is the best month. You can shuck your own oysters or buy them pre-shucked in jars at seafood markets. Look for the extra-small size.

• • ● • •

MAKES 8 SERVINGS

Dipping Sauce
½ cup mayonnaise
1 tablespoon fresh lemon juice
2 teaspoons Worcestershire sauce

• • ● • •

1 cup all-purpose flour
1 cup medium-ground yellow cornmeal
¼ teaspoon chili powder
¼ teaspoon salt
¼ teaspoon freshly ground pepper
1 cup peanut or canola oil
24 extra-small oysters, preshucked and drained in a colander (don't rinse)

● To prepare the dipping sauce, whisk together the mayonnaise, lemon juice, and Worcestershire sauce. Refrigerate until ready to serve.

● To prepare the oysters, in a medium-sized bowl, combine the flour, cornmeal, chili powder, salt, and pepper. Mix well with a whisk and set aside.

● When you are ready to cook the oysters, heat the oil in a 10- or 12-inch cast iron skillet until the temperature reads 350°F on a deep-fry thermometer. (You can also test the heat by sprinkling a small bit of flour into the oil; it should bubble immediately.)

● Dredge the oysters in the flour mixture, shake off the excess flour, and carefully place 6 at a time in the hot oil. (You can also use a slotted spoon or a deep-fryer basket to lower them into the oil.) Fry until golden brown, about 2 minutes. Transfer to paper towels. Repeat with the remaining oysters. Serve hot with the dipping sauce.

DUNGENESS CRAB QUESADILLAS WITH AVOCADO-LIME SAUCE

The iron skillet is the best way to cook quesadillas quickly and evenly. We love quesadillas cut into wedges and served as an appetizer or a quick lunch. You can cook cheese quesadillas in your skillet over a campfire or outdoor grill and serve with the Avocado-Lime Sauce.

• • • • •

MAKES 8 SERVINGS

Avocado-Lime Sauce
1 ripe avocado, peeled and chopped
Juice of 1 lime
1 tablespoon lemon juice
1 cup sour cream

Quesadillas
8 ounces Dungeness crabmeat
1 cup grated cheddar cheese
1/2 cup diced red bell pepper
1/4 cup chopped green onion
1/2 cup mayonnaise
1 teaspoon fresh lemon juice
8 flour tortillas, 8 inches in diameter

• • • • •

Avocado slices, for garnish
Lime wedges, for garnish

• To prepare the sauce, place the avocado, lime juice, lemon juice, and sour cream in a blender and purée until smooth. Refrigerate until ready to serve. (You can prepare the sauce up to 1 hour in advance.)

• Position a rack in the center of the oven and preheat to 200°F.

• To prepare the quesadillas, mix together the crabmeat, cheese, bell pepper, green onions, mayonnaise, and lemon juice in a large bowl. Lay out 4 of the tortillas and spread evenly with the crab mixture. Top with the remaining tortillas.

● Warm a 10- or 12-inch cast iron skillet over medium-low heat. Place one quesadilla in the skillet and cook for 2 minutes, until the tortilla starts to brown, then turn and cook on the other side until the cheese melts and the filling is warm. Transfer to a platter and keep warm in the oven. Repeat with the remaining quesadillas.

● Cut the quesadillas into wedges and drizzle lightly with the Avocado-Lime Sauce. Serve on small plates with sliced avocado and lime wedges.

GARLIC SPICED PRAWNS

We find that when we purchase prawns with their shells on, they retain more of their true flavor. If you prefer, you can use shelled and deveined prawns. If you do keep the tails on, provide your guests with a bowl for the tails and plenty of napkins. You don't have to marinate the prawns, but they are more flavorful if you do.

• • ● • •

MAKES 4 SERVINGS

⅛ teaspoon ground turmeric
⅛ teaspoon cayenne
¼ teaspoon ground coriander
⅛ teaspoon paprika
¼ teaspoon curry powder
2 teaspoons fresh thyme leaves, lightly chopped
⅛ teaspoon salt
Grated zest of 1 lemon
5 tablespoons butter
2 cloves garlic, minced
Juice of 1 lemon
1 pound medium-sized prawns, heads and shells removed, tails attached

• • ● • •

Lettuce leaves, for serving
Lemon slices, for garnish
1 tablespoon chopped flat-leaf parsley, for garnish

● In a small bowl, mix together the turmeric, cayenne, coriander, paprika, curry powder, thyme, salt, and lemon zest. In a 10- or 12-inch cast iron skillet, melt the butter over low heat. Stir in the spice mixture and garlic. Increase the heat to medium-low and cook for 1 minute.

● Add the prawns to the skillet and cook for 2 to 3 minutes; turn all the prawns over and cook for 2 minutes more. Squeeze the lemon juice over the prawns. Transfer to a large platter lined with lettuce leaves, garnish with lemon slices and parsley, and serve.

EGGPLANT-PEPPER TAPENADE

Known as zaalouk *in Morocco and shared with us by our friend Meriem Atowani Kass, this tapenade is traditionally served as a side dish to chicken with preserved lemons. (See page 71 for our version using Cornish game hens.) You can also serve this as an appetizer or add it to tomato sauce and toss with pasta.*

• • ● • •

MAKES 6 TO 8 SERVINGS (ABOUT 2 CUPS)

1 red or green bell pepper
1 tablespoon extra virgin olive oil
1 tablespoon canola oil
1 large eggplant, peeled and julienned
3 cloves garlic, minced
1 tablespoon chopped fresh cilantro
1 teaspoon paprika
¼ teaspoon salt

• • • • •

Warm pitas, for serving

To roast the bell pepper, place it directly on the burner on a gas stove over medium-high heat or in a cast iron skillet over medium-high heat. Roast, turning occasionally, until the skin blackens, about 10 minutes. Transfer to a paper bag for 10 minutes to loosen the skin and cool the pepper. Remove from the bag and wipe the pepper with a damp paper towel to remove the skin. Make a cut in the pepper to release the steam. Slice in half; remove the stem, seeds, and white vein; and then julienne.

Heat the olive oil and canola oil in a 10- or 12-inch cast iron skillet over medium-low heat. Add the roasted pepper strips, eggplant, garlic, cilantro, paprika, and salt and cook, stirring occasionally, for 30 minutes. The eggplant will release all of its liquid and the mixture will become a thick sauce. Remove from the heat and serve with warmed pitas.

ENTRÉES

Rosemary-Crusted Rack of Lamb

Lamb Chops with Pomegranate Glaze

Stir-Fried Flank Steak

Monday Night Meatloaf

Seared Beef Tenderloin with Veal Demi-Glace

Braised Spareribs in Merlot Sauce

Schultz Sunday Supper Pot Roast

Open-Face Sloppy Joes

Slow-Roasted Beef Brisket with Apple Cider–Ginger Barbecue Sauce and Caramelized Sweet Onions

No-Fail Beef Stew

Seared Pork Chops with Plum-Mustard-Cornichon Sauce

Fennel-Seared Pork Tenderloin with Blackberry Sauce

Smoked Pork Chops with Apples, Fresh Thyme, and Sweet Onions

Tom's Brick Chicken

Chicken Paillards with Red and Yellow Peppers and Kalamata Olives

Skillet-Roasted Chicken with Rosemary, Garlic, and Maple Balsamic Glaze

Chicken with Herbed Dumplings

Cornish Game Hens with Preserved Lemons and Olives

Grandpa Don's Picnic Fried Chicken

Chicken with Calvados and Cream

Pan-Seared Chicken with Sausage, Fingerling Potatoes, and Green Beans

Quick-to-Fix Roasted Chicken Hash

Pan-Seared Duck Breasts with Orange-Thyme Sauce

Mussels, Prawns, and Halibut in Coconut Curry Sauce

Pan-Seared Wild King Salmon with Dill Tartar Sauce

Baked Halibut with Fresh Fennel and Cucumber-Fennel Raita

Pan-Seared Sea Scallops with Apple-Thyme Sauce

Garlic Roasted Dungeness Crab

Dungeness Crab Cakes with Tarragon Aïoli

Pan-Seared Trout with Almonds

Shellfish Paella

Tamale Pie

Bernie's Cabbage Rolls

Cornish Pasty

Classic Grilled Reuben

41

ooking in a cast iron skillet goes hand in hand with bringing everyone to the table together. Family and friends inspired many of our recipes, and many of them we created together, side by side in the kitchen, doing what we love most—preparing foods meant to be shared with loved ones. The Slow-Roasted Beef Brisket with Apple Cider–Ginger Barbecue Sauce and the Schultz Sunday Supper Pot Roast are perfect for long, leisurely weekend evenings. On busy weeknights quick, tasty meals are best: We love to serve our family Open-Face Sloppy Joes, Tom's Brick Chicken, or Pan-Seared Wild King Salmon. For special meals we enjoy Seared Beef Tenderloin with Veal Demi-Glace, Chicken Paillards with Red and Yellow Peppers and Kalamata Olives, or the wonderfully delicious and fun to eat Garlic Roasted Dungeness Crab. Whatever the occasion, when you have good food hot out of a cast iron skillet, you have a meal to share and remember.

The following cooking methods respond best to cast iron's dry, even heat.

Braising and stewing are ideal for the tough muscle cuts of meat, such as chuck roast, short ribs, shanks, shoulder meat, and stew meat. It is important to brown the meat first and then add the amount of liquid specified in the recipe. The browning and caramelizing of the outside of the meat is best done in a heated cast iron pan with a little oil or butter. When you try to brown and caramelize in a nonstick skillet, excess moisture develops, which prevents browning and tightens and toughens the meat.

Pan-searing in a cast iron skillet creates a flavorful brown crust on tender cuts of meat such as pork chops, steaks, and pork tenderloins or fish fillets. To pan-sear, season the meat or fish with salt and pepper. Heat the skillet over medium-high heat, add a little olive oil, and sear both sides of the meat in the skillet. Then place the skillet with the meat or fish into a preheated 375°F oven and finish cooking according to the recipe. When pan-searing fish, scallops, skinless chicken, or pork, wait until a golden crust forms. If you force any of these prematurely from the pan, they will stick.

Browning in cast iron prevents excess moisture from developing. Ground beef actually browns and crisps, rather than stewing and becoming flavorless and gray as it does in other types of pans. If the only thing you do is brown ground beef in your cast iron pan, you'll be happy you have it.

Stir-frying works best over medium-high heat. Be sure to have all of your ingredients chopped, sliced, and diced, and ready to add to your hot skillet. Heat the pan over medium-high heat, then add your oil, swirling it around to distribute evenly. You want to keep your ingredients moving around in the pan continuously, using a wooden spatula or tongs. Sautéing in an iron skillet browns and caramelizes meats and vegetables beautifully. For gas or electric stove top ranges, a 12- or 14-inch flat-bottomed skillet can substitute for a wok.

Sautéing is a gentle approach to cooking, using medium heat. As with stir-frying, sautéing in an iron skillet browns and caramelizes meats and vegetables perfectly.

ROSEMARY-CRUSTED RACK OF LAMB

The rack is the rib section of the lamb. There are usually seven or eight rib bones. In this recipe two racks of lamb are cooked in the oven and sliced into individual chops. It's hard to resist the temptation to pick up the lamb chops to get every bite of meat. Serve the lamb with oven-roasted potatoes and spring asparagus.

• • • • •

MAKES 4 SERVINGS

> ⅔ cup fresh white bread crumbs
> 1 tablespoon chopped fresh rosemary
> 1 tablespoon chopped fresh parsley
> ¼ cup (½ stick) salted butter, melted
> 2 racks standard domestic lamb, trimmed of all fat
> Salt and freshly ground black pepper
> 2 tablespoons Dijon mustard, divided

• • • • •

Hot pepper jelly or fresh mint sauce, for serving

● Position a rack in the oven 8 inches from the broiler and preheat the broiler.

● In a medium bowl, mix together the bread crumbs, rosemary, parsley, and melted butter. Set aside.

● Season the racks of lamb with salt and pepper. Place them in a 12-inch cast iron skillet, meat side up, interlocking both sets of ribs in the center of the skillet. Cover the bone ends with pieces of foil, and place the pan in the oven. Partially close the oven door and broil for 8 to 10 minutes.

● Remove the pan from the oven and reduce the heat to 325°F. Brush each rack with 1 tablespoon Dijon mustard. Spread the bread crumb mixture evenly over both racks. Return the pan to the oven, but this time place it on the middle rack and roast for 20 to 25 minutes. Remove from the oven, cover the rack loosely with foil, and let rest for 3 to 5 minutes. Cut in between rib bones and serve each person 3 to 4 lamb chops. Serve with hot pepper jelly or fresh mint sauce.

LAMB CHOPS WITH POMEGRANATE GLAZE

The tartness of the pomegranate molasses is balanced by the honey in the marinade, which mellows the strong flavor lamb can sometimes have. The lamb chops sear beautifully and cook quickly in the iron skillet. Serve with couscous and roasted vegetables.

• • • • •

MAKES 4 SERVINGS

¼ cup pomegranate molasses (see note)
¼ cup honey
½ cup red wine
¼ cup plus 3 tablespoons extra virgin olive oil
2 cloves garlic, minced
1 teaspoon ground coriander
12 individual lamb rib chops (buy 6 two-rib chops and cut them in half)
Salt and freshly ground black pepper

⁕ Position a rack in the center of the oven and preheat to 350°F.

⁕ In a medium bowl, mix together the pomegranate molasses, honey, red wine, ¼ cup olive oil, garlic, and coriander. Place the rib chops in a 9- x 12-inch glass baking dish, pour the marinade over the top, and sprinkle with salt and pepper. Cover with plastic wrap and refrigerate for 2 to 3 hours, turning the chops over a couple of times.

⁕ Heat 1 tablespoon of the remaining olive oil in a 10- or 12-inch cast iron skillet over medium-high heat. Working in batches of 4 chops at a time, brown the chops on both sides, adding 1 tablespoon more oil for each batch. Transfer to a baking sheet. Repeat with the remaining 2 batches.

⁕ When all of the chops are on the baking sheet, place it in the oven and bake for 10 minutes for medium-rare or 15 minutes for medium. Remove from the oven, cover the chops with foil, and let the meat rest for 5 minutes.

⁕ To serve, place 3 chops on each plate.

Note: **Pomegranate molasses is available at specialty grocery stores.**

STIR-FRIED FLANK STEAK

The cast iron skillet acts just like a wok and caramelizes the beef strips in this Asian-style dish with flavors of soy and ginger. Have all of your ingredients ready before cooking. Keeping the food moving in the pan is the secret to a successful stir-fry.

• • ● • •

MAKES 4 SERVINGS

5 tablespoons soy sauce
5 tablespoons orange juice
2 cloves garlic, peeled and minced
½ teaspoon crushed red pepper flakes
2 teaspoons fresh ginger, peeled and grated
2 teaspoons Chinese five-spice powder
1 teaspoon cornstarch
¼ cup sugar
2 teaspoons sesame oil
1 pound flank steak
2 tablespoons vegetable oil
½ red bell pepper, seeded and cut into ½-inch strips
½ yellow bell pepper, seeded and cut into ¼-inch strips
½ red onion, cut crosswise into ¼-inch crescent slices
4 ounces sugar snap peas, cut in half at an angle

• • ● • •

Steamed rice, for serving

● To prepare the sauce, in a small bowl, combine the first 9 ingredients (soy sauce through sesame oil) and set aside.

● Cut the flank steak in half lengthwise, then cut diagonally, crosswise, into ½-inch-wide strips.

● Heat the vegetable oil in a 12-inch skillet over medium-high heat. Add the beef strips and stir-fry for 2 minutes. Add the bell peppers, onion, and peas. Stir-fry for 1 minute. Add the sauce mixture and stir-fry until the sauce starts to bubble, about 2 minutes more. Serve immediately over steamed rice.

MONDAY NIGHT MEATLOAF

This recipe makes enough for a weekend family dinner, sandwiches the next day, and meatloaf hash for a weeknight dinner.

• • ● • •

MAKES 8 SERVINGS

2 tablespoons salted butter
1 cup chopped yellow onion (about 1 medium-sized onion)
1 cup fresh bread crumbs
1 pound extra-lean ground beef
½ pound ground pork
1 can (8 ounces) tomato sauce
2 large eggs
1 cup grated cheddar cheese
1 teaspoon salt
½ teaspoon freshly ground black pepper
2 teaspoons dried Italian herb seasoning

• • ● • •

Ketchup, for serving

● Position a rack in the center of the oven and preheat to 350°F.

● In a 10- or 12-inch cast iron skillet, melt the butter over medium heat. Stir in the chopped onion and cook for 3 minutes. Transfer to a large mixing bowl. Place all of the remaining ingredients in the bowl with the onions, and mix together with your hands until well blended. Form into a football-shaped loaf in the same skillet in which you cooked the onions.

● Place the skillet in the oven and bake until the center is no longer pink, about 1 hour. Let cool for 10 minutes. Pour off the excess fat and juices. Slice and serve hot, with ketchup for dipping.

SEARED BEEF TENDERLOIN WITH VEAL DEMI-GLACE

Demi-glace is a highly concentrated, flavorful sauce. Making a demi-glace would normally take all day, and we don't know very many people who have that kind of time to cook. When we discovered premade demi-glaces, our problem was solved. These demi-glaces are the real thing, rich and flavorful. Serve this at a dinner party and your guests will feel very special. Try it with mashed potatoes or polenta to soak up the sauce, along with green beans or Skillet-Roasted Asparagus (see page 107).

• • ● • •

MAKES 4 SERVINGS

Sauce
2 tablespoons salted butter, divided
1 tablespoon finely chopped shallots
¾ ounce veal demi-glace (see Resources, page 158)
¼ cup water
¼ cup red wine
2 tablespoons marsala wine or port
¼ teaspoon chopped fresh rosemary
1 bay leaf
Salt and freshly ground black pepper

• • ● • •

4 beef tenderloin fillets (8 ounces each)
Salt and freshly ground black pepper
1 tablespoon extra virgin olive oil

● Position a rack in the center of the oven and preheat to 350°F.

● To prepare the sauce, melt 1 tablespoon of the butter in a small saucepan over medium-low heat. Add the shallots and cook, stirring occasionally, until softened, about 3 minutes. Reduce the heat to low. Whisk in the demi-glace and the water, stirring until the demi-glace has dissolved. Whisk in the wine, marsala, rosemary, bay leaf, salt, and pepper. Whisk in the remaining tablespoon of butter. Simmer over low heat while preparing the steaks, or remove from the heat and reheat just before serving.

To prepare the steaks, season on both sides with salt and pepper. Heat the olive oil in an 8-, 10-, or 12-inch cast iron skillet over medium-high heat for 2 minutes. Add the steaks and sear on each side until golden brown, about 4 minutes per side. Transfer the skillet to the oven and cook for 15 minutes for medium-rare, 20 minutes for medium, and 25 to 30 minutes for well done.

Remove the skillet from the oven. Remove steaks from the pan and wrap with aluminum foil. Let stand for 5 minutes. Remove the bay leaf from the sauce. Transfer the steaks to plates and pour some sauce over each one. (You can pour the sauce through a small sieve first if you prefer to leave out the shallots and rosemary.)

BRAISED SPARERIBS IN MERLOT SAUCE

This recipe was inspired by our friend Frank Wesner, who uses beef short ribs. We decided to try a leaner version using the country-style spareribs. There is no need for a knife—the meat is fork tender and melts in your mouth. For the canned tomatoes, we like Muir Glen fire-roasted tomatoes for their depth of flavor; however, regular canned or fresh tomatoes also work well. Serve these ribs with Horseradish Mashed Potatoes (recipe follows).

• • • • •

MAKES 6 SERVINGS

3 pounds country-style pork spareribs
Salt and freshly ground black pepper

Merlot Sauce

1 medium yellow onion, coarsely chopped (about 1 cup)
6 to 8 cloves garlic, coarsely chopped
2 cans (14.5 ounces each) Muir Glen fire-roasted crushed tomatoes or
   regular crushed tomatoes (drain off excess liquid)
¼ cup light brown sugar
1 cup merlot or other full-bodied red wine
⅔ cup balsamic vinegar
½ teaspoon salt
½ teaspoon freshly ground black pepper

• Position a rack in the center of the oven and preheat to 350°F.

• To prepare the ribs, rinse them, pat dry with a paper towel, and season with salt and pepper on both sides. Place a 12-inch cast iron skillet over medium-high heat; add the ribs, fat side down. Cook, turning once, until browned on all sides, 2 to 3 minutes. Transfer the ribs to a plate, and drain and reserve all but 2 tablespoons fat from the skillet.

• To prepare the sauce, turn down the heat to medium-low, add the onions to the skillet, and cook, stirring occasionally, until they start to soften, about 5 minutes. Add the garlic and cook for 2 minutes. Stir in the tomatoes, brown sugar, red wine, balsamic vinegar, salt, and pepper.

Turn the heat up to medium and bring the sauce to a boil. Return the spareribs to the skillet, pushing them down gently to submerge. Protecting both hands with oven mitts, cover tightly with foil. The liquid will reduce while cooking, leaving a rich, flavorful sauce. With the oven mitts, carefully place the skillet in the middle of the oven and bake until the meat breaks apart easily with a fork, about 1½ to 2 hours.

Accompaniment: **Horseradish Mashed Potatoes**
> 2 pounds russet or Yukon Gold potatoes, peeled and quartered
> ½ teaspoon salt, plus more for seasoning
> 6 tablespoons heavy cream or half-and-half
> 3 tablespoons unsalted butter
> 3 tablespoons mascarpone or sour cream
> 1 tablespoon creamy horseradish
> Freshly ground black pepper

Place the potatoes in a large stockpot with the ½ teaspoon salt and enough water to cover. Bring to a rapid boil over high heat. Reduce the heat to medium and cook until soft; drain. Return the potatoes to the pot and cook over medium heat for 3 to 5 minutes, allowing them to absorb some of the moisture. Reduce the heat to low and shake the potatoes over the heat for 3 minutes. Mash with a potato ricer, using medium-wide holes.

In a small saucepan over low heat, mix together the cream, butter, mascarpone, and horseradish. Cook for 5 minutes. Be careful not to let this mixture come to a boil.

Slowly pour the cream mixture into the potatoes while whipping the potatoes with a fork or a whisk. Mix until light and fluffy. Season to taste with salt and pepper and serve hot.

SCHULTZ SUNDAY SUPPER POT ROAST

In Missoula, Montana, Sunday dinner at our cousin's home is a family affair. The pot roast cooks slowly on top of the stove until it is fork-tender and the onions have melted down to make a wonderful gravy. You need to use a deeper skillet, one with 4-inch sides, or a cast iron Dutch oven. The semi-dry roasting in this recipe develops the rich flavor of the meat.

• • • • •

MAKES 6 SERVINGS

1 tablespoon extra virgin olive oil
1 chuck roast, 3½ pounds
Salt and freshly ground black pepper
1 medium yellow onion, thinly sliced
1 cup boiling water

Gravy
2 tablespoons all-purpose flour
½ cup water
Additional 1½ cups water, or ½ cup water and 1 cup heavy cream

• To prepare the pot roast, heat the olive oil in a 4-inch-deep, 10- or 12-inch cast iron skillet over medium-high heat. Season with salt and pepper. Place the roast in the skillet and brown for 5 minutes on each side. Add the onions and boiling water. Cover tightly with a lid and simmer gently over low heat until tender, about 2 hours. (Or, alternatively, cover and bake at 325°F for 2½ hours.)

• To make gravy from the juices, transfer the meat to a platter and keep warm. In a small bowl, whisk together the flour and the ½ cup water until well blended. Stir the mixture into the juices in the pan. Cover and cook over medium-low heat, stirring, until the sauce thickens. Gradually add the 1½ cups water (or, for a delicious creamy gravy, add ½ cup water and 1 cup heavy cream), and continue to stir until smooth and thickened. Spoon over the sliced pot roast.

Note: **Cold leftover pot roast, chopped with sweet yellow onions and mixed with a little horseradish and mayonnaise, makes a great sandwich spread.**

OPEN-FACE SLOPPY JOES

When you want something quick to serve your family, Open-Face Sloppy Joes please all ages. The ground beef browns so well in the cast iron skillet. Serve with Crispy Slaw (recipe follows).

• • ● • •

MAKES 4 SERVINGS

1 tablespoon vegetable oil
1 tablespoon salted butter
1 cup chopped yellow onion (about ½ onion)
½ cup chopped red bell pepper (about ½ pepper)
12 ounces lean ground beef
2 cups tomato sauce
¼ cup ketchup
1 to 2 teaspoons Worcestershire sauce
4 small hamburger buns, toasted and buttered

● Heat the oil and butter in a 10- or 12-inch cast iron skillet over medium heat. Add the chopped onions and cook, stirring occasionally, for 5 minutes. Add the bell pepper and ground beef, stirring to crumble and brown the meat. Add the tomato sauce, ketchup, and Worcestershire sauce and simmer for 15 minutes.

● Place a toasted bun, open face, buttered side up, on each plate and spoon the meat mixture over the top.

Accompaniment: **Crispy Slaw**

MAKES 4 TO 6 SERVINGS

½ head green cabbage, finely shredded
¼ cup white wine vinegar
3 tablespoons mayonnaise
1 tablespoon sugar
Salt and freshly ground black pepper

● Place the shredded cabbage in a large bowl. Cover with cold water and 8 to 10 ice cubes. Let crisp for 1 hour. Make the dressing by mixing the vinegar, mayonnaise, and sugar together. Drain the cabbage in a colander. Transfer to a serving bowl and coat with the dressing. Sprinkle with salt and pepper to taste.

SLOW-ROASTED BEEF BRISKET WITH APPLE CIDER–GINGER BARBECUE SAUCE AND CARAMELIZED SWEET ONIONS

This is comfort food at its best! Slow-simmered with a sweet-and-sour sauce that has a hint of ginger, the meat becomes very tender. Use any leftovers from this dish for Beef Brisket Hash with Yukon Gold Potatoes (see page 16).

• • • • •

MAKES 4 TO 6 SERVINGS

Apple Cider–Ginger Barbecue Sauce
³/₄ cup brown sugar
1 cup ketchup
¹/₂ cup apple cider vinegar
1 tablespoon Worcestershire sauce
¹/₄ cup soy sauce
1 clove garlic, minced
1-inch piece fresh ginger, peeled and grated

Caramelized Onions
2 tablespoons extra virgin olive oil, plus more as needed
¹/₂ sweet yellow onion, cut into quarters, then thinly sliced crosswise

• • • • •

1 beef brisket, 1 to 3 pounds

● To prepare the barbecue sauce, place the brown sugar, ketchup, apple cider vinegar, Worcestershire sauce, soy sauce, garlic, and ginger in a medium saucepan. Simmer over medium-low heat for 10 minutes. Refrigerate until ready to use.

● Position a rack in the center of the oven and preheat to 300°F.

● To prepare the onions, spread the olive oil evenly in a 12-inch cast iron skillet over medium heat, add the onions, and cook, stirring occasionally, until golden. Remove from the pan and set aside.

● Turn up the heat to medium, add the brisket, and cook, turning once, until seared on both sides, about 5 minutes. You may need to add a bit more olive oil to keep the meat from sticking to the pan.

● Remove from the heat and spread the barbecue sauce evenly over the top of the meat. Sprinkle the cooked onions over the brisket, cover the skillet tightly with foil, and bake until fork-tender, about 3 hours. To serve, cut crosswise into ½-inch slices.

NO-FAIL BEEF STEW

The key to successful beef stew is to make the beef melt-in-your-mouth tender. You first need to brown it well, which a cast iron pan does perfectly. When the stew is simmering, you don't want to add excess moisture to it by allowing condensation to form on the lid. To prevent this, wrap the lid in a dish towel (the corners should be on top of the lid) before placing it tightly on the skillet. Serve this stew over mashed potatoes or polenta.

• • • • •

MAKES 6 TO 8 SERVINGS

2 pounds beef stew meat

½ teaspoon salt

¼ teaspoon freshly ground black pepper

4 to 5 tablespoons extra virgin olive oil, divided

8 ounces white or cremini mushrooms, cleaned, stems trimmed, and quartered

1 yellow onion, diced

2 stalks celery, halved lengthwise and sliced ¼ inch thick

2 large carrots, peeled and cut diagonally into 2-inch-thick slices

2 cloves garlic, minced

1 teaspoon fresh thyme leaves, or ½ teaspoon dried thyme

2 cans (14.5 ounces each) crushed tomatoes, with their juice (see note)

1 cup full-bodied red wine (such as cabernet sauvignon)

1½ cups water

2 bay leaves

1 tablespoon Worcestershire sauce

¼ to ½ cup pitted or unpitted green olives

• • • • •

3 tablespoons fresh chopped parsley, for garnish

● Season the meat with the salt and pepper. Heat 1 tablespoon of the olive oil in a deep 12-inch cast iron skillet or Dutch oven over medium-high heat. Working in 3 or 4 batches, add the beef to the pan and cook, browning on all sides, for about 5 minutes. Transfer the browned beef to a plate, add another tablespoon of olive oil to the pan, and add the next batch of beef. You need to work quickly between batches so that the meat bits in the pan don't blacken. Repeat with the remaining batches.

* Reduce the heat to medium and add 1 tablespoon olive oil to the pan. Add the mushrooms, onions, celery, carrots, garlic, and thyme. Cook, stirring occasionally, for 5 minutes. Return the beef to the pan and stir in the tomatoes and their liquid, wine, water, and bay leaves. Bring to a light boil, then reduce the heat to low. Cover (see the note at the beginning of the recipe) and simmer for 1 hour.

* Add the Worcestershire sauce and olives and cook, covered, for another 20 to 30 minutes. Remove the bay leaves.

* If the stew seems to have too much liquid and you would like to thicken it, place a large strainer over a large bowl and pour the stew into the strainer to drain off the liquid. Move the strainer to another bowl and set aside. Pour the stew liquid back into the pan and bring to a boil over medium-high heat until it starts to thicken. Do not reduce for too long or the sauce will become too salty. Return the beef and vegetables to the pan, warm, and serve garnished with parsley.

Note: **We like Muir Glen fire-roasted crushed tomatoes. If you can't find them, just add ½ teaspoon paprika to regular crushed tomatoes. You can also substitute canned chopped tomatoes for most recipes.**

SEARED PORK CHOPS WITH PLUM-MUSTARD-CORNICHON SAUCE

Known in Burgundy, France, as côtes de porc vigneronnes (grape growers' pork chops), this succulent and elegant dish is traditionally served after a day spent harvesting grapes. Susan Herrmann Loomis, a chef, teacher, and cookbook author who lives in France, inspired this recipe. It has the perfect balance of salty and sweet from the plums, capers, and cornichons.

• • ● • •

MAKES 6 SERVINGS

Plum-Mustard-Cornichon Sauce

2 tablespoons salted butter
1 large shallot, minced (about 3 tablespoons)
1 large clove garlic, minced
½ cup water
1 tablespoon capers, mashed or lightly chopped
2 tablespoons plum butter (see note)
2 tablespoons minced cornichons (about 4 cornichons) (see note)
1 tablespoon Dijon mustard
Salt and freshly ground black pepper

• • ● • •

2 tablespoons butter, divided
2 tablespoons extra virgin olive oil, divided
6 pork loin rib chops, ¾ inch thick, with the bone in (8 to 10 ounces each)
Salt and freshly ground black pepper

• • ● • •

2 tablespoons chopped fresh parsley, for garnish

● Position a rack in the center of the oven and preheat to 350°F.

● To prepare the sauce, melt the butter in a small saucepan over medium-low heat. Add the shallots, garlic, and water to the pan and cook for 2 minutes. Whisk in the capers, plum butter, cornichons, and mustard. Season to taste with salt and pepper. Set aside.

To prepare the pork chops, melt 1 tablespoon of the butter with 1 tablespoon of the olive oil in a 10- or 12-inch skillet over medium heat. Season the pork chops with salt and pepper. Add 3 chops to the skillet and cook, turning once, until lightly browned, about 3 minutes on each side. Transfer to a plate and set aside. Repeat with the 3 remaining pork chops, adding 1 more tablespoon each of butter and olive oil to the skillet.

When all of the pork chops are browned, place them in the skillet and transfer to the oven. (You may need to use 2 skillets to fit all 6 chops; add 1 tablespoon each of butter and olive oil to the second skillet before adding the pork.) Bake until a meat thermometer inserted into the center of the chops registers 150°F, about 8 minutes. (The pork will continue to cook after it is removed from the oven.) Transfer the pork chops to a warm serving platter and cover lightly with foil to keep warm. If the pork chops have released any juices onto the platter, add them to the sauce. Heat the sauce over low heat and whisk briefly, then pour the warm sauce over the pork chops. Garnish with parsley and serve.

Note: **Cornichons are tiny, brine-packed French pickles. They are available at most large grocery stores and specialty grocery stores, where you can also find plum butter. To make your own plum butter, just place 6 to 8 pitted prunes in a blender together with 3 tablespoons hot water, and purée until smooth.**

FENNEL-SEARED PORK TENDERLOIN WITH BLACKBERRY SAUCE

This technique of pan-searing meat in the skillet and then finishing it in the oven keeps the meat moist and tender. The searing creates a crust, which seals in the juices. Make the sauce first and then cook the tenderloin. The sweetness of the onions and the tartness of the blackberries complement the savory flavor of the fennel-rubbed pork.

• • • • •

MAKES 4 SERVINGS

Fennel Salt
2 tablespoons fennel seed
4 teaspoons sea salt

Blackberry Sauce
2 tablespoons salted butter
½ medium yellow onion, thinly sliced and cut into 1-inch pieces
2 teaspoons Dijon mustard
1 cup chicken stock
2½ cups fresh or frozen blackberries
¼ cup honey

• • • • •

1 pork tenderloin, about 1 pound
2 tablespoons extra virgin olive oil

• Position a rack in the center of the oven and preheat to 350°F.

• To prepare the fennel salt, spread the fennel seed in a cast iron skillet and roast in the oven for 6 minutes. Grind in a spice grinder, and then mix with the sea salt in a small bowl.

• Increase the oven heat to 375°F.

• To prepare the blackberry sauce, melt the butter in a medium saucepan over medium heat. Add the onions and cook, stirring occasionally, for 5 minutes. Stir in the mustard. Add the chicken stock and cook, stirring, for several minutes. Add the blackberries and honey, reduce the heat to medium-low, and simmer until the sauce begins to thicken, about 10 minutes. Strain half of the sauce into a bowl, reserving the juices. Add these juices back to the remaining sauce in the pan. Discard the berries and onions left in the strainer.

● To prepare the pork, rub the tenderloin evenly with 1 tablespoon of the fennel salt. Place a 10- or 12-inch cast iron skillet over medium-high heat. Add the olive oil and let it heat for 1 minute. Add the tenderloin and cook until browned on all sides, about 6 minutes. Place the skillet in the oven and roast, uncovered, for 20 minutes. Remove from the oven and let rest for several minutes. Pour any excess juice from the cooked tenderloin into the Blackberry sauce. Reheat the sauce quickly. Slice the tenderloin crosswise, arrange on a platter, and spoon the warm blackberry sauce over the top.

SMOKED PORK CHOPS WITH APPLES, FRESH THYME, AND SWEET ONIONS

A perfect fall dinner—savory and sweet. You can find smoked pork chops in specialty meat markets. For the apples, we like to use the Honeycrisp, Granny Smith, or Fuji varieties. The smoky, salty flavor of the pork chops is complemented by the sweet apples. Serve with Rosemary Roasted Potatoes (see page 103). You'll find smoked pork chops at most grocery stores.

• • • • •

MAKES 4 SERVINGS

   1 tablespoon extra virgin olive oil
   ½ medium sweet yellow onion, very thinly sliced
   3 apples, peeled, quartered, and cored
   1 teaspoon fresh thyme leaves, or ½ teaspoon dried thyme
   ½ teaspoon salt
   4 smoked pork chops, ½ inch thick

• Heat the oil in a 10- or 12-inch cast iron skillet. Add the onions and cook over medium heat for 5 minutes, stirring occasionally. Slice the apples crosswise into ½-inch-thick slices and add to the onions. Add the thyme and salt.

• Place a square of parchment paper directly on top of the apples. Simmer on top of the stove over medium-low heat for 10 minutes. Meanwhile, preheat the oven to 350°F.

• Remove the parchment paper and place the smoked pork chops on top of the apples. Cover with aluminum foil. Using a fork, poke holes in the foil 4 or 5 times. Place the skillet in the oven and bake for 18 minutes. Serve immediately.

TOM'S BRICK CHICKEN

Tom Kramis likes to fix chicken for his family this way. Ask your butcher to remove the backbone so the chicken will lie flat. Use a foil-wrapped brick or another, smaller cast iron skillet wrapped in foil and placed on top of the chicken to weight it down while cooking. This flattens the chicken and crisps the skin. If you can, use free-range chicken, as it is more moist and tender. Serve with oven-roasted potatoes and steamed asparagus.

• • • • •

MAKES 4 SERVINGS

    1 teaspoon finely chopped fresh rosemary
    1 teaspoon fresh oregano, lightly chopped
    1 teaspoon fresh thyme leaves
    1 teaspoon sea salt
    1 whole chicken, 2½ pounds, split at the backbone and flattened
    Freshly ground black pepper
    ¼ cup extra virgin olive oil

● Preheat oven to 400°F.

● Mix the herbs with the salt in a small bowl, and rub the herb mixture over the skin side of the chicken. Heat the olive oil in a 10- or 12-inch skillet over medium heat. Place the chicken in the skillet, skin side down. Weight the chicken down with a foil-wrapped brick or a second smaller skillet. Cook for 15 minutes, then place in the oven and continue cooking for 30 minutes longer.

● Carve the chicken into pieces and serve.

CHICKEN PAILLARDS WITH RED AND YELLOW PEPPERS AND KALAMATA OLIVES

The peppers, capers, olives, and lemons in this dish are colorful on the plate, and their flavors all blend together to form a delicious sauce for the chicken. Have everything ready ahead of time, and then quickly sauté and serve when it's time to eat.

• • • • •

MAKES 4 SERVINGS

4 boneless, skinless chicken breast halves (2 whole chicken breasts cut in half)

3 tablespoons extra virgin olive oil, divided

1 medium red bell pepper, seeds and ribs removed, sliced into ½-inch strips

1 medium yellow bell pepper, seeds and ribs removed, sliced into ½-inch strips

¼ cup all-purpose flour

1 teaspoon salt

½ teaspoon freshly ground black pepper

1 tablespoon salted butter

⅓ cup kalamata olives, pitted

1 tablespoon capers, rinsed and drained

1 to 2 tablespoons fresh lemon juice

• • • • •

Chopped fresh parsley, for garnish

● Preheat the oven to 250°F and place 4 dinner plates in the oven to warm.

● Place the chicken breasts, one at a time, in a large zip-lock bag (slightly opened), and pound lightly with a mallet or rolling pin until flattened to ⅜ inch thick.

● Warm 2 tablespoons of the olive oil in a 10- or 12-inch cast iron skillet over medium heat. Add the pepper strips and cook, stirring occasionally, for 3 minutes. Transfer to a small plate and set aside.

● Mix the flour, salt, and pepper in a flat dish. Lightly coat the chicken breasts in the flour mixture, shaking off any excess flour. Heat the butter and 1 tablespoon olive oil in the skillet over medium heat until the butter melts. Add the chicken breasts and cook until golden brown on one side, about 3 minutes. Turn and cook until golden brown on the other side, about 3 minutes longer.

● Transfer to a warm serving platter. Sprinkle the peppers, olives, capers, and lemon juice over the chicken. Garnish with chopped parsley and serve.

SKILLET-ROASTED CHICKEN WITH ROSEMARY, GARLIC, AND MAPLE BALSAMIC GLAZE

We love the flavor and moistness of this chicken. The inside stays moist and the outside crispy and flavorful. Serve with braised greens or a green salad. Use leftovers for sandwiches or as a tasty pizza topping along with Mama Lil's Sweet Peppers (see Resources, page 158).

• • • • •

MAKES 4 TO 7 SERVINGS

2 tablespoons fresh rosemary (about 5 sprigs), plus 5 more whole rosemary sprigs
2 cloves garlic
Grated zest of 1 lemon (reserve ½ of the lemon to roast in the chicken)
¼ cup olive oil
¼ cup balsamic vinegar
¼ cup maple syrup
1 tablespoon lemon juice
1 whole chicken, 3 to 4 pounds
2 pounds red potatoes, scrubbed and halved if small, or quartered if large
Salt and freshly ground black pepper

● Position a rack in the center of the oven and preheat to 400°F.

● Using a mortar and pestle, crush together the 2 tablespoons rosemary, garlic, and lemon zest until they form a paste. Place the paste in a bowl and whisk in the olive oil, balsamic vinegar, maple syrup, and lemon juice. (You can also use a blender for this step. Place the rosemary, garlic, lemon zest, vinegar, maple syrup, and lemon juice in a blender and blend until combined. With the blender running, drizzle in the olive oil.)

● Remove the neck and giblets from the chicken, then rinse the chicken and pat dry. Rub the body and neck cavity with salt and pepper. Using your fingers, loosen the skin and rub the rosemary mixture under the skin over the breast, thighs, and drumsticks. Halve the lemon you used for zesting and place half in the cavity, along with the 5 whole rosemary sprigs.

Place the potatoes in a 10- or 12-inch cast iron skillet. Season with salt and pepper, then place the chicken, breast side up, on top of the potatoes. Roast in the oven for 55 to 65 minutes for a 4-pound bird. (Add 8 minutes for each additional pound.) After 20 minutes, baste the chicken with the pan juices. Repeat 20 minutes later. Roast until a meat thermometer inserted in the thickest part of the thigh, without touching a bone, reads 170° to 175°F and the juices run clear. If you want the dark meat to be fork-tender, roast to 180°F.

Remove the chicken from the pan and place it on a sheet of foil to rest for 5 minutes. (You can return the potatoes to the oven and reduce the heat to 300°F to keep them warm.) Meanwhile, reduce the pan juices slightly. After carving the chicken, place it on warmed plates with the potatoes. Spoon some of the reduced pan juices over the top, and serve.

CHICKEN WITH HERBED DUMPLINGS

This recipe is a family favorite for a wintertime Sunday dinner, served with a fresh green salad. The herbs in the moist dumplings and the coarse salt on top really set this dish apart. The dumplings usually disappear first, but we like to serve the leftover chicken and vegetables over mashed potatoes the next day.

• • • • •

MAKES 6 TO 8 SERVINGS

2 pounds boneless, skinless chicken breast halves

Salt and freshly ground black pepper

3 tablespoons olive oil, divided

3 tablespoons unsalted butter

½ yellow onion, peeled and diced

4 ounces small white mushrooms, cleaned, stems trimmed, and halved

1 shallot, peeled and thinly sliced

¼ cup all-purpose flour

3 cups chicken stock

¾ cup heavy cream

¼ cup dry sherry

4 medium carrots, peeled and cut into ½-inch slices

2 celery stalks, cut into ½-inch pieces

1 bay leaf

¼ teaspoon ground or freshly grated nutmeg

1 teaspoon finely chopped fresh oregano leaves

1 teaspoon finely chopped fresh thyme leaves

¾ cup frozen peas

Herbed Dumplings

1¼ cups all-purpose flour
⅔ cup cornmeal
2½ teaspoons baking powder
½ teaspoon salt
7 tablespoons chilled butter
3 teaspoons chopped fresh rosemary
1 cup whole milk
½ teaspoon kosher salt or fleur de sel

● Position a rack in the center of the oven and preheat to 425°F.

● To prepare the chicken, rinse the chicken breasts, pat them dry, and cut them into 1-inch strips. Season with salt and pepper and divide into 3 batches. Heat 1 tablespoon of the olive oil in a 10- or 12-inch cast iron skillet over medium-high heat. Add the first batch of chicken and cook, turning once, until browned on both sides, about 5 minutes. Transfer to a cutting board and repeat with the remaining 2 batches, adding another tablespoon of olive oil for each batch. Set the chicken aside.

● In the same skillet, melt the butter over medium heat. Add the onion, mushrooms, and shallot and cook, stirring occasionally, until the onions have softened, about 5 minutes. Stir in the flour. Slowly add the chicken stock, cream, and sherry, whisking often, and bring to a boil over medium heat. Reduce the heat and add the carrots, celery, bay leaf, nutmeg, oregano, and thyme. Generously season to taste with salt and pepper and simmer for 5 minutes. Return the chicken strips to the skillet and cook over medium heat for 5 minutes. Mix in the peas.

● To prepare the dumplings, whisk together the flour, cornmeal, baking powder, and salt in a large bowl. Cut the chilled butter into tablespoon-sized slices. Using a pastry blender and working quickly so the butter remains cold, cut in the butter until the pieces are pea-sized. (You can also transfer the flour mixture to a food processor fitted with a steel blade, add the butter, and pulse 5 or 6 times.) Gently mix in the rosemary, using your hands or a spatula. Add the milk and mix gently just until the ingredients are wet and slightly sticky.

● Using a large spoon, scoop up some of the dumpling mixture and drop it on top of the chicken mixture. Repeat until all the dumpling mixture is used (you should have about 10 dumplings). Sprinkle the tops with the kosher salt and return the skillet to the oven. Bake until the dumplings are golden brown, 20 to 25 minutes. If you want to brown the tops of the dumplings more, brush the tops with melted butter and turn on the broiler for the last few minutes, keeping a close eye on the dumplings at this point. Serve from the skillet.

THE
CAST IRON
SKILLET
COOKBOOK

CORNISH GAME HENS WITH PRESERVED LEMONS AND OLIVES

Our friend Meriem Atowani Kass brought this recipe with her when she moved to Seattle from Casablanca. The olives and preserved lemons, a combination commonly used in Moroccan cooking, are a delicious addition to game hens. In Morocco, this dish is presented surrounded by many small dishes, such as Eggplant-Pepper Tapenade (see page 39) and fresh tomato salsa. You can also serve this dish on top of a bed of couscous. Buy preserved lemons at a specialty grocery store, or see the recipe on page 73 to prepare your own.

• • ● • •

MAKES 2 TO 4 SERVINGS

1 yellow onion, coarsely chopped

¼ cup chopped fresh cilantro, or 2 teaspoons ground coriander

2 cloves garlic, minced

2 teaspoons ground ginger

½ teaspoon saffron

½ teaspoon paprika

¼ cup olive oil

Juice of 2 lemons

1 cup water

2 Cornish game hens, cut into fourths (or substitute chicken: 2 breasts and 2 thighs, and 2 legs with or without skin)

Salt and pepper

1 cup green Greek olives (about 20 olives), pitted or unpitted

Peel of ½ preserved lemon, cut into ½-inch-thick slices

• • ● • •

3 tablespoons chopped fresh cilantro, for garnish

● Position a rack in the center of the oven and preheat to 350°F.

● In a large bowl, mix together the first 8 ingredients (onion, cilantro, ginger, garlic, saffron, paprika, olive oil, and lemon juice). Working in batches, place the game hen in the large bowl with the sauce and toss to coat. Heat a 10- or 12-inch skillet over medium-high heat. Add 3 to 4 pieces of game hen at a time. Do not crowd the pan! Brown for 3 minutes on each side. Remove to a plate and continue in the same manner with the rest of the game hen. Return all pieces to the skillet and pour the onion mixture and water over the top, coating them well. Place the skillet over medium heat for 10 minutes. Transfer the skillet to the oven and bake, uncovered, for another 35 minutes.

• Meanwhile, place the olives and preserved lemon peel in a separate small saucepan. Add ¼ cup of the game hen sauce from the skillet. Bring to a boil and heat olives all the way through.

• Remove the skillet from the oven and transfer the game hen pieces to a plate. Set aside. Place the skillet over medium-high heat and bring the sauce to a boil until it begins to thicken, about 5 minutes.

• To serve, pour the sauce from the skillet over the game hen. Garnish with the olives and lemon peel and any of the sauce that remains. Sprinkle with the cilantro and serve.

Preserved Lemons

We love to have a jar of preserved lemons standing by. They are a salty yet sweet, very fragrant addition to lamb or fish. They are surprisingly simple to make and also are a lovely gift. You can add whole cloves or whole allspice to the jar to give these golden gems a new dimension.

● ● ● ● ●

½ cup salt
¼ cup water
6 ripe lemons

● Quarter lemons lengthwise and place in a large bowl. Mix together with the salt and water. Stir until the salt has dissolved. Transfer the lemons into a 1-quart sterilized Mason jar with a tight-fitting lid. Pour the remaining saltwater mixture into the jar to cover the lemons. Screw the lid on tightly and let sit for 7 days, at room temperature, until the lemon peels become soft and brownish yellow. Shake the jar occasionally. For storage, add olive oil, cover, and refrigerate. They will last for months. Rinse the lemons before using.

GRANDPA DON'S PICNIC FRIED CHICKEN

Grandpa loves to picnic. At any outdoor event, he brings his cooler filled with fried chicken, potato salad, and watermelon. While his potato salad (recipe follows) isn't a skillet recipe, we always serve the two together.

• • ● • •

MAKES 6 SERVINGS

3½ pounds chicken pieces, skin removed (cut the breast pieces in half crosswise)
1 tablespoon salt, plus more for seasoning
2 teaspoons freshly ground black pepper, plus more for seasoning
2 cups all-purpose flour
Canola oil, for frying

● Wash the chicken and dry thoroughly with paper towels. Season lightly with salt and pepper. Place the flour, 1 tablespoon salt, and 2 teaspoons pepper in a medium-sized paper bag. Shake to mix. Add half of the chicken pieces, close the bag tightly, and shake gently to coat the chicken. Transfer the chicken to a rack and repeat with the remaining chicken.

● Pour the oil into a 12-inch cast iron skillet to a depth of ¼ inch. Heat over medium heat. Carefully place the chicken pieces into the warm oil, standing back in case it spatters. (We like to use a spatter guard, available at cookware shops. See Resources, page 158.) Cook until the chicken is golden brown on one side. Turn and brown the other side. Remove the skillet from the burner and pour off the excess oil from the pan. Lower the heat to medium-low. Return the skillet to the heat and cover, leaving the lid partially ajar to prevent excess steaming. Cook for 40 minutes more. Remove the chicken from the pan and serve at room temperature, or cool in the refrigerator and then pack into a plastic container with a tight-fitting lid and place in a cooler with ice packs.

Accompaniment: **Grandpa Don's Potato Salad**

    2 pounds Yukon Gold potatoes, well scrubbed
    8 ounces sweet onions, thinly sliced and then chopped
    4 hard-boiled eggs, peeled
    1 cup mayonnaise, plus more as needed
    1 tablespoon Colman's dry mustard
    Salt and freshly ground black pepper

Place the potatoes in a deep stockpot, cover with water, and boil until tender. Drain and let cool to room temperature. Peel the potatoes and cut into bite-sized pieces. Place in a medium bowl. Sprinkle the chopped onions over the top, cover with plastic wrap, and refrigerate until well chilled.

When ready to serve, cut up the eggs and add to the potatoes. Add the mayonnaise and mustard and mix well. Add more mayonnaise if you want a creamier consistency. Season to taste with salt and pepper.

CHICKEN WITH CALVADOS AND CREAM

Calvados is a wonderful apple brandy that is made in the Pays d'Auge region of Normandy, France. The brand most commonly found in the United States is Grand Solage Boulard, which is made with up to 120 varieties of apples. We always have a bottle on hand to flavor sauces for pork, duck, and mussels or to mix into homemade ice cream.

• • • • •

MAKES 4 TO 6 SERVINGS

3 tablespoons extra virgin olive oil, divided
3 tablespoons butter, divided
3 yellow onions, cut into 1/4-inch-thick slices
1 whole chicken, 3 1/2 to 4 pounds, separated into 2 breasts, 2 thighs, 2 wings, and 2 legs
Sea salt
Freshly ground black pepper
2 apples (Jonagold or Gala), peeled, cored, and cut into 2-inch-thick slices
1/4 cup Calvados
1/4 cup heavy cream
1/2 cup chicken stock
6 fresh thyme sprigs
1 bay leaf

• • • • •

2 tablespoons chopped fresh flat-leaf parsley, for garnish

● Position a rack in the center of the oven and preheat to 400°F.

● Heat 1 tablespoon olive oil and 1 tablespoon butter in a 10- to 12-inch cast iron skillet over medium heat. Add the onions and cook, stirring occasionally, for 10 minutes, until softened but not browned. Transfer to a plate and set aside.

• Return the skillet to the heat and increase the heat to medium-high. Heat 1 tablespoon of the olive oil in the skillet. Season the chicken with sea salt and pepper. Add half of the chicken pieces to the skillet and cook, turning occasionally, until golden brown on all sides. Transfer to a plate. Repeat with the second batch of chicken, adding the remaining tablespoon of olive oil. Set the chicken aside.

• Reduce the heat to medium. Add the remaining 2 tablespoons butter to the skillet. Add the apples and cook, stirring occasionally, until lightly golden and just slightly soft, about 5 minutes. Stir in the Calvados, cream, chicken stock, and thyme sprigs. Return the onions and chicken to the pan, mixing gently. Add the bay leaf.

• Place the skillet in the oven and bake for 20 minutes. Turn over all the chicken pieces and cook until the chicken is a deep golden brown and the juices run clear, about 20 minutes longer. Remove from the oven; sprinkle with parsley, salt, and pepper. Serve hot.

PAN-SEARED CHICKEN WITH SAUSAGE, FINGERLING POTATOES, AND GREEN BEANS

Serve this one-dish meal right in the skillet. The flavors complement each other and create delicious juices to spoon over the top of each serving.

• • • • •

MAKES 4 SERVINGS

1 pound fingerling potatoes
8 ounces small green beans, stem ends removed
4 tablespoons extra virgin olive oil, divided
4 bone-in chicken breasts, skin removed
Salt and freshly ground black pepper
1 cup finely chopped yellow onion
1 clove garlic, minced
12 ounces smoked andouille sausage, cut into ¼-inch-thick slices
½ red bell pepper, cut into thin strips
½ cup chicken stock

• Boil the potatoes in a stockpot until tender. Drain and let cool. Cut in half lengthwise and set aside.

• Pour an inch of water into a shallow pan and bring to a boil. Add the green beans. Cover and cook just until they start to soften, 3 to 5 minutes. Drain the beans and spread out onto paper towels to cool.

• Warm a 10- or 12-inch cast iron skillet over medium-high heat. Add 2 tablespoons of the olive oil. Season the chicken breasts with salt and pepper and cook for 4 minutes on each side. Transfer to a platter and reserve.

• Add the remaining 2 tablespoons olive oil to the skillet and reduce the heat to medium. Add the onions and garlic to the pan and cook, stirring occasionally, until soft. Add the sausage to the skillet and cook for several minutes. Add the cooked potatoes and green beans. Mix together with a spatula. Cut each chicken breast in half crosswise and place on top of the potatoes and beans. Sprinkle the bell pepper strips over the top. Add the chicken stock. Cover loosely with aluminum foil, reduce the heat to medium-low, and cook for 12 to 15 minutes. Serve from the skillet.

QUICK-TO-FIX ROASTED CHICKEN HASH

After a long day at work, nothing is easier than picking up a freshly roasted chicken at the grocery store to make this simple, flavorful chicken hash for dinner. Serve with a green salad and crusty bread. No other pan will brown a hash like a cast iron pan. Use the leftover chicken to make soup for lunch the next day.

• • ● • •

MAKES 4 SERVINGS

¼ cup (½ stick) salted butter

1½ cups chopped sweet yellow onion

6 cups peeled, diced, and cooked Yukon Gold potatoes, about 2 pounds (½-inch cubes)

4 cups roast chicken, cut into small pieces

¾ cup heavy cream, divided

Salt and freshly ground black pepper

• • ● • •

¼ cup chopped fresh parsley, for garnish

Melt the butter in a 10-inch cast iron skillet over medium heat. Add the onions and cook, stirring occasionally, for 5 minutes. Add the potatoes. Stir and continue to cook for 5 minutes. Add the chicken, mix well, and continue to cook for several minutes more. Pour ½ cup of the cream over the top of the chicken mixture. Season to taste with salt and pepper. Cook until nice and hot, 3 to 5 minutes longer. Pour the remaining ¼ cup cream over the top. Sprinkle with the parsley, season again with salt and pepper, and serve.

PAN-SEARED DUCK BREASTS WITH ORANGE-THYME SAUCE

Leaving the skin on the duck breast gives duck its wonderful flavor, adding a delicious, salty crispiness. If you don't have time to make the rub, you can just salt and pepper the skin because the sauce is so flavorful. You can also double or triple the spice rub and keep it on hand for your next duck, chicken, or pork dinner. Duck breasts are available in the frozen section of specialty grocery stores.

• • ● • •

MAKES 4 SERVINGS

Spice Rub

2 teaspoons kosher salt or fleur de sel

1 tablespoon light brown sugar

2 teaspoons fennel seed

1 tablespoon fresh rosemary

2 teaspoons coriander seed, or 1 teaspoon ground coriander

½ teaspoon ground ginger

1 teaspoon fresh oregano

2 large sage leaves

1 teaspoon fresh thyme leaves

½ teaspoon grated lemon zest

• • ● • •

4 boneless, skin-on duck breasts, about 2 pounds

Orange-Thyme Sauce

¼ cup dry sherry

¼ cup sherry vinegar

2 tablespoons orange juice

½ cup low-sodium chicken stock

2 teaspoons honey

1 teaspoon coarsely chopped leaves

1 tablespoon unsalted butter

- To prepare the rub, combine the salt, brown sugar, fennel seed, rosemary, coriander seed, ginger, oregano, sage, thyme, and lemon zest in a coffee or spice grinder and grind until smooth. You can use a mortar and pestle if you don't have an electric grinder.

- Position a rack in the center of the oven and preheat to 425°F.

- To prepare the duck, rinse the breasts and pat dry. Trim any extra skin from the meat side of the breasts, leaving a ¼-inch overhang on the edges. Pull the tendon out of the breast, and pat the tender back into place. With a sharp knife, score the skin in a crosshatch pattern, making 6 to 8 cuts, ½ inch deep, in one direction and another 6 to 8 cuts in the other direction. Try not to cut through the meat. Coat both sides of the duck breasts with the spice rub mixture.

- Heat a 10- or 12-inch cast iron skillet over medium-high heat for 1 minute. Add the duck breasts to the skillet, skin side down, and sear for 1 minute. Spoon out any excess duck fat from the pan and discard. Reduce the heat to medium-low and continue to cook for 3 to 4 minutes, rendering much of the duck fat. The skin should be crisp and golden brown.

- Turn the breasts over and cook for 1 minute, spooning any excess fat from the pan, then place the skillet in the oven. Roast until the duck is cooked to your liking—3 to 4 minutes for medium-rare (135°F on a meat thermometer). Cook a few minutes longer for medium. (Make sure not to cook the duck for too long, or it will toughen.) Transfer the duck to a plate and cover with aluminum foil to keep warm.

- To prepare the sauce, wipe the excess fat from the skillet with a paper towel, and place the skillet over medium-high heat. Add the sherry, sherry vinegar, and orange juice, scraping up the browned bits and stirring them into the sauce. Boil until slightly reduced. Add the chicken stock, honey, and thyme and bring to a gentle boil until slightly reduced again, about 2 minutes. Reduce the heat to low and whisk in the butter.

- Slice the duck ½ inch thick. Serve on warm plates, and spoon about 3 tablespoons of sauce over each serving.

MUSSELS, PRAWNS, AND HALIBUT IN COCONUT CURRY SAUCE

We love the way the seafood takes on the wonderful flavors of the sauce in this recipe. The mussels are perfectly plump, the prawns crisp, and the fish firm. There is enough extra sauce to pour over your rice.

• • ● • •

MAKES 4 TO 6 SERVINGS

2 cups canned coconut milk

¼ cup vegetable oil

1 to 2 tablespoons red curry paste (adjust to your heat preference)

1½ tablespoons fish sauce

1 teaspoon dark brown sugar

½ teaspoon salt

1 stalk lemongrass, white part only, cut in half lengthwise

4 fresh kaffir lime leaves (see note)

1 pound fresh mussels, scrubbed and debearded

8 ounces fresh or frozen tiger prawns, peeled and deveined

1½ pounds fresh halibut fillets, skin removed, cut in half lengthwise, then into thirds

Leaves from 10 sprigs fresh cilantro

10 fresh Thai basil or other basil leaves, stems removed and coarsely chopped

• • ● • •

Cooked jasmine rice, for serving

1 lime, cut into 6 to 8 wedges, for garnish

● Skim ¼ cup of the thick cream from the top of the coconut milk and set aside. Stir the remaining cream in with the thinner milk.

● Heat the oil and reserved coconut cream in a 10- to 12-inch cast iron skillet over medium heat until bubbling. Add the curry paste, increase the heat to medium-high, and stir-fry until the oil separates and the paste is lightly browned. Lower the heat to medium and stir in the fish sauce, brown sugar, and salt. Add the coconut milk, lemongrass, and kaffir lime leaves. Bring to a boil, stirring occasionally.

● Add the mussels and prawns and cook for 3 to 4 minutes. Then add the halibut and continue cooking until the mussels open, the prawns turn pink, and the halibut is white throughout, 4 to 5 minutes more.

● Remove the lemongrass and kaffir lime leaves. Scatter the cilantro and basil over the top. Serve in individual bowls over the jasmine rice, with the lime wedges on the side.

Note: **If you cannot find fresh kaffir lime leaves, you can substitute 2 teaspoons of fresh lime juice.**

PAN-SEARED WILD KING SALMON WITH DILL TARTAR SAUCE

In the Pacific Northwest, we are fortunate to be able to get wild king salmon year round, either fresh or expertly frozen at sea. Here is an easy way to cook it indoors for a fast dinner. Simply sear the salmon in the skillet and finish cooking it in the oven.

• • • • •

MAKES 4 SERVINGS

Dill Tartar Sauce

½ cup mayonnaise
⅓ cup finely diced dill pickle
⅓ cup finely diced red onion
1 tablespoon fresh lemon juice
¼ teaspoon dried dill weed

Salmon Rub

1 teaspoon sea salt
½ teaspoon freshly ground black pepper
2 tablespoons brown sugar
1 teaspoon lemon zest

• • • • •

4 wild salmon fillets, 6 ounces each and 1 inch thick, skin removed
2 tablespoons extra virgin olive oil

● To prepare the Dill Tartar Sauce, in a small bowl mix together the mayonnaise, pickle, onion, lemon juice, and dill weed. Cover and chill.

● Position a rack in the center of the oven and preheat to 400°F.

● For the rub, combine the sea salt, pepper, brown sugar, and lemon zest. Sprinkle the rub over the top side of the salmon, then gently pat with your fingers to distribute evenly. Heat the olive oil in a 10- or 12-inch skillet over medium-high heat. Place the salmon fillets in the skillet and cook for 2 minutes. Carefully turn over and cook for 2 minutes on the other side.

● Transfer the skillet to the oven and bake until the fish flakes easily when tested with a fork, about 6 minutes. Serve with the Dill Tartar Sauce.

Ebelskivers (*Scandinavian Pancakes*), *page* 10

Zucchini-Onion Frittata, *page* 13

Pecan Sticky Buns, *page* 22

Queso Fundido Verde, *page 28*

Garlic Spiced Prawns, *page 38*

Chicken with Herbed Dumplings, *page 68*

Fried Flank Steak, *page 46*

Garlic Roasted Dungeness Crab, *page 88*

Fennel-Seared Pork Tenderloin with Blackberry Sauce, *page 60*

Ginger-Glazed Carrots, *page* 118

Fennel-Ricotta Skillet Bread, *page* 112

Cornbread Pudding, *page 115*

Old-Fashioned Peach Dumplings with Nutmeg Cream, *page* 144

Plum Galette, *page* 154

Bing Cherry Clafouti, *page 152*

Seafood Bake, *page* 130

BAKED HALIBUT WITH FRESH FENNEL AND CUCUMBER-FENNEL RAITA

The best halibut is available March through November. Firm and moist, it lends itself well to baking. Here, it is complemented nicely by the fresh cucumber sauce. Since asparagus season also begins in March, asparagus makes an excellent springtime accompaniment.

● ● ● ● ●

MAKES 4 SERVINGS

Cucumber-Fennel Raita

1 cup sour cream
½ cup diced cucumber (¼-inch pieces)
½ cup diced fennel bulb (¼-inch pieces)
1 teaspoon chopped fresh mint leaves
¼ teaspoon salt
¼ teaspoon coarsely ground black pepper

● ● ● ● ●

1 fresh fennel bulb, thinly sliced
4 halibut fillets, 6 to 8 ounces each and 1 inch thick, skin removed
½ cup extra virgin olive oil
1 lemon, thinly sliced
1 tablespoon finely chopped fresh thyme leaves
1 teaspoon sea salt

❧ To prepare the raita, mix together the sour cream, cucumber, fennel, mint, salt, and pepper in a medium bowl and refrigerate until ready to serve.

❧ To prepare the fish, position a rack in the center of the oven and preheat to 375°F.

❧ Place the sliced fennel in a 10- or 12-inch cast iron skillet. Lay the halibut fillets on top of the fennel and drizzle with the olive oil. Scatter the lemon slices, thyme, and sea salt over the top. Cover with foil and bake until the fish flakes easily when tested with a fork, 15 to 20 minutes. Serve with Cucumber-Fennel Raita.

PAN-SEARED SEA SCALLOPS WITH APPLE-THYME SAUCE

We love to sear scallops in a hot cast iron skillet—it turns them golden and succulent. The sweetness of the apples with the ginger and thyme complements the scallops' sweet flavor. For a salad variation of this recipe, see the note on the next page.

• • ● • •

MAKES 4 SERVINGS

Apple-Thyme Sauce
¼ cup apple cider
½ cup chicken stock
3 sprigs fresh thyme
3 tablespoons white wine
1 teaspoon Pernod
¼-inch slice fresh ginger, peeled and cut in half
3 tablespoons chilled butter, cut into 3 pieces

• • ● • •

1 tablespoon extra virgin olive oil
1 tablespoon butter
16 large sea scallops

● Preheat the oven to 250°F and place 4 small, flat bowls or salad plates in the oven to warm.

● To prepare the sauce, place the cider, chicken stock, thyme sprigs, wine, Pernod, and ginger in a small saucepan over high heat. Bring to a boil and cook until reduced by half. Remove the thyme and the ginger slices. Turn the heat down to low and whisk in the butter, 1 tablespoon of at a time. Maintain the lowest heat or remove the sauce from the heat while preparing the scallops.

● To prepare the scallops, place the olive oil and butter in a 10- or 12-inch cast iron skillet over medium heat. Heat for 2 minutes. Add the scallops to the pan and brown for 2 minutes on each side. Place 4 scallops in each warmed bowl and ladle about ¼ cup of sauce over the scallops in each bowl. Serve immediately.

Note: You can also add these scallops to a salad. After searing them, cut each scallop in half horizontally. To prepare the Apple-Thyme Sauce as a dressing, omit the chicken stock. Follow the instructions for reducing the sauce and then, instead of whisking in the butter, remove from the heat, let cool, and whisk in $\frac{1}{4}$ cup olive oil. Toss with mixed greens, then top the salad with the scallops, sliced apples, and toasted pecans.

GARLIC ROASTED DUNGENESS CRAB

We like our crab chilled and plain in the Northwest. Big bowls of cracked Dungeness crab are as good as it gets. But for special occasions we sometimes dress it up this way because the crab flavor still shines through.

• • ● • •

MAKES 2 SERVINGS

¼ cup extra virgin olive oil
4 cloves garlic, finely chopped
¼ cup finely minced fresh parsley
1 teaspoon sea salt
1 Dungeness crab, cooked, cleaned, and broken into pieces
Melted butter, for dipping

● Position a rack in the center of the oven and preheat to 400°F.

● Pour the olive oil into a 10- or 12-inch cast iron skillet. Add the garlic, parsley, and sea salt. Stir over medium heat for 3 minutes. Add the crab and stir to coat evenly with the garlic mixture. Place the skillet in the oven and bake for 10 minutes. Serve with warm melted butter for dipping and plenty of napkins!

DUNGENESS CRAB CAKES WITH TARRAGON AÏOLI

Crunchy on the outside, smooth and creamy on the inside, these crab cakes are a delicious way to use fresh Dungeness crabmeat for a simple but elegant dinner. The sweet flavor of the crab is complemented by the tangy aïoli. The crab cakes need to chill for at least 2 hours before cooking, so you'll want to plan ahead. Serve with your favorite coleslaw.

• • • • •

MAKES 12 CRAB CAKES

Tarragon Aïoli

1 egg
¼ teaspoon Colman's dry mustard
2 tablespoons fresh lemon juice
1 tablespoon fresh tarragon leaves (about 3 sprigs)
1 cup light olive oil
Salt and freshly ground black pepper

Crab Cakes

¼ cup (½ stick) salted butter
½ cup finely diced yellow onion (about ½ onion)
¼ cup finely chopped red bell pepper (about ½ pepper)
1 tablespoon Dijon mustard
¼ cup chopped fresh parsley
½ cup mayonnaise
1 pound Dungeness crabmeat
1 tablespoon fresh lemon juice
¼ teaspoon Tabasco sauce
½ teaspoon Worcestershire sauce
½ cup soft bread crumbs
2 cups panko bread crumbs, or other coarse bread crumbs
Butter and vegetable oil, for frying

● To prepare the aïoli, put the egg, dry mustard, lemon juice, and tarragon in a food processor or a blender and process briefly. Then, with the machine running on low speed, add the oil in a slow, steady stream until the mixture thickens. Season to taste with salt and pepper. Cover with plastic wrap and refrigerate until ready to serve.

• To prepare the crab cakes, melt the butter in a 10- or 12-inch cast iron skillet over low heat. Add the onion and bell pepper and cook for 5 minutes. Remove from the heat and let cool. Transfer to a glass bowl. Stir in the mustard, parsley, and mayonnaise. Add the crabmeat, lemon juice, Tabasco sauce, Worcestershire sauce, and soft bread crumbs and mix gently to combine. Refrigerate the mixture for at least 2 hours.

• After chilling, shape the crab mixture into 12 small, round cakes, 3 inches in diameter and ¾ inch thick. Place the panko crumbs in a shallow dish and press each cake into the crumbs, coating completely on both sides.

• In the same skillet over medium heat, heat enough butter and oil to coat the bottom of the pan. Fry the crab cakes in batches until golden brown, 2 to 3 minutes on each side. If necessary, place the finished crab cakes on a paper towel–lined baking sheet and keep warm in a 250°F oven until ready to serve. Serve with the aïoli.

PAN-SEARED TROUT WITH ALMONDS

Good trout is available year-round. Our favorite preparation is this traditional French dish, which combines the nutty flavors of the almonds and browned butter with the fresh trout. Serve with oven-roasted fingerling potatoes.

• • • • •

MAKES 4 SERVINGS

4 trout fillets
Salt and freshly ground black pepper
¼ cup all-purpose flour
6 tablespoons (¾ stick) salted butter
¼ cup sliced almonds
4 tablespoons crème fraîche (see note) or sour cream

• • • • •

Lemon slices, for garnish
2 tablespoons chopped flat-leaf parsley, for garnish

- Position a rack in the center of the oven and preheat to 250°F.

- Season the tops of the trout fillets with salt and pepper. Place the flour in a flat dish and dredge the fillets in the flour.

- Melt the butter in a 10- or 12-inch cast iron skillet over medium-low heat. Add the fish and cook for 4 minutes on each side. Transfer to a platter and keep warm in the oven.

- Place the almonds in a separate small sauté pan over medium-low heat. Cook, stirring occasionally, until light brown. Stir in the crème fraîche and season lightly with salt and pepper. Cook until the sauce begins to brown lightly, 3 to 5 minutes. Pour over the top of the trout fillets, garnish with lemon slices and chopped parsley, and serve immediately.

Note: **You can find crème fraîche at specialty grocery stores or make your own simple version: Mix 1 cup heavy cream and ½ cup sour cream until combined. Cover and refrigerate.**

SHELLFISH PAELLA

This classic dish from Spain provides the perfect background for Northwest shellfish. The saffron gives the whole dish a beautiful golden color.

• • • • •

MAKES 6 SERVINGS

1 teaspoon saffron threads
¼ cup white wine
4 tablespoons extra virgin olive oil, divided
4 bone-in skinless chicken breast halves (2 whole chicken breasts)
6 bone-in skinless chicken thighs
1 large yellow onion, chopped (about 2 cups)
2 cloves garlic, finely chopped
½ pound chorizo sausage
2 cups paella rice
1 teaspoon smoked paprika (see note, page 93)
1 teaspoon chopped fresh rosemary
2½ cups chicken stock
1 can (14.5 ounces) Muir Glen fire-roasted chopped tomatoes, drained
1 pound fresh mussels, scrubbed and debearded
½ pound medium prawns, peeled and deveined (thawed if frozen)
½ cup frozen peas, thawed

• • • • •

1 tablespoon chopped fresh parsley, for garnish
1 lemon, cut into wedges, for garnish

● In a small bowl, dissolve the saffron in the white wine.

● Heat 2 tablespoons of the olive oil in a 12-inch cast iron skillet over medium heat. Brown the chicken breasts and thighs about 5 pieces at a time and cook, turning occasionally, until browned on all sides, about 10 minutes. Transfer to a plate and repeat with the next batch of chicken.

● Add the remaining 2 tablespoons olive oil to the skillet, then add the onions and garlic and cook, stirring occasionally, for 3 to 5 minutes. Remove the casing from the chorizo and break into pieces. Cook for 3 minutes, crumbling the sausage with a wooden spoon as it cooks. Add the rice, paprika, rosemary, and saffron (with the white wine), and stir to mix and coat the rice. Pour the chicken stock and tomatoes over the rice. Stir the mixture once to incorporate (it's important not to overmix).

● Arrange the browned chicken pieces on top. Bring to a boil, then reduce the heat and simmer for 30 minutes. Then scatter the mussels, prawns, and peas over the rice (do not stir). Cover tightly with aluminum foil and continue to cook until the rice is tender, mussels are open, and prawns are pink, about 5 minutes longer.

● Remove from the heat, garnish with the parsley and lemon wedges, and serve.

Note: **Smoked paprika is best for this recipe, but if you can't find it easily, you can substitute regular paprika.**

TAMALE PIE

For a long time we were on the search for the perfect tamale pie. Here, we've added ground beef, chili, our favorite Muir Glen tomatoes, and fresh spices. For a vegetarian option you can add black beans and a vegetarian chili. It's a one-pan meal!

• • ● • •

MAKES 8 SERVINGS

Topping
Moist Cornbread (see recipe on page 109)

Filling
1 pound lean ground beef

2 teaspoons ground cumin

2 teaspoons chili powder

Salt and freshly ground black pepper

1 white onion, diced

2 cloves garlic, minced

2 cans (14.5 ounces each) Muir Glen fire-roasted crushed tomatoes (see note, page 57)

2 cans (14.5 ounces each) mild or hot chili

2 tablespoons diced green chiles (optional)

½ cup fresh or frozen corn, thawed and drained if frozen

2 cups grated sharp cheddar cheese

2 tablespoons melted salted butter

• • ● • •

Sour cream, for serving

¼ cup chopped fresh cilantro, for serving

● Position a rack in the center of the oven and preheat to 400°F.

● Prepare the Moist Cornbread batter on page 109, but do not bake it. Set batter aside and continue with this recipe.

● To prepare the filling, heat a 10-inch cast iron skillet over medium-high heat. Add the ground beef, cumin, chili powder, salt, and pepper and cook, stirring occasionally, until the beef is browned. Transfer to a plate.

- Reduce the heat to medium. Add the onion and garlic to the skillet and cook, stirring occasionally, until the onion is softened but not browned, about 5 minutes.

- Add the beef back to the skillet with the onion mixture. Add the tomatoes, chili, green chiles (if using), and corn.

- Sprinkle the cheddar cheese over the top. Pour the cornbread batter over the top of the cheese, spreading it evenly with a spatula. Transfer the skillet to the oven and bake for 15 minutes. Remove the pan from the oven and drizzle the melted butter over the top. Return the skillet to the oven and continue to bake until the top is nicely browned and a toothpick inserted in the center comes out clean, 15 to 20 minutes. Remove from the oven and let stand for 10 minutes. Cut into wedges and serve with sour cream and cilantro.

BERNIE'S CABBAGE ROLLS

Bernie and Bob Manofsky shared this recipe, which has been passed down in their family for three generations, with us. We cooked it together during a visit, and it immediately became part of our family's repertoire.

• • • • •

MAKES ABOUT 16 ROLLS

2 heads green cabbage
1 pound lean ground beef
8 ounces lean ground pork
½ cup uncooked long-grain rice
½ yellow onion, grated (about ½ cup)
1 clove garlic, minced
1 teaspoon ground cinnamon
2 teaspoons salt
1 teaspoon freshly ground black pepper
½ cup tomato juice
3 cups chicken broth
1 can (14.5 ounces) diced tomatoes, drained

• • • • •

Sour cream, for serving

◦ Position a rack in the center of the oven and preheat to 350°F.

◦ Set the cabbages down on a cutting surface so that the base is facing up. Insert a long knife just next to the core and cut all around it, removing the large end of the core. Add water to a large saucepan to a depth of 2 inches. Place the cabbages in a steamer basket in the pan, cover, bring to a boil, and steam until the leaves are soft enough to be removed, about 3 minutes. Separate the large outer leaves and let cool on paper towels; you will use only 6 large outer leaves per head. Slice the rest of one head of cabbage and place in the bottom of a 12-inch cast iron skillet. (Save the other head of cabbage for another use.)

● In a medium bowl, combine the beef, pork, rice, onion, garlic, cinnamon, salt, pepper, and tomato juice. Mix well.

● Place ⅓ cup of the meat mixture on the stem end of each cabbage leaf. Roll once, then fold in the sides and continue to roll. Place seam side down in the skillet on top of the sliced cabbage. Repeat until all of the meat mixture is used.

● Pour in the chicken broth, cover with foil, and bake for 50 minutes. Carefully remove pan from the oven and drain off half of the liquid. Spoon the tomatoes evenly over the cabbage rolls. Replace the foil and bake for 10 minutes longer.

● Serve from the skillet and top each roll with sour cream.

CORNISH PASTY

The Welsh copper miners in Butte, Montana, carried these meat pies in their lunch pails. Baked in a skillet and served for dinner with a green salad, they're a way we celebrate our family's Montana roots. The meat pies look like large, golden-brown turnovers.

• • ● • •

MAKES 4 SERVINGS

Pastry
2 cups all-purpose flour
½ teaspoon salt
¾ cup vegetable shortening
½ cup very cold water

Filling
1 to 2 russet potatoes, peeled and diced into ½-inch cubes (about 3 cups)
¾ cup chopped yellow onion (about ½ onion)
1 pound top sirloin, cut into ½-inch cubes
2 teaspoons salt
½ teaspoon freshly ground black pepper
2 tablespoons salted butter, divided

• • ● • •

Ketchup, for serving

● To prepare the pastry, mix together the flour and salt in a large bowl. With your fingers, mix in the shortening until the mixture has the consistency of coarse cornmeal. Add the water and stir with a fork until it starts to stick together. Form into a ball, divide in half, and shape each half into a flat disk, ½ inch thick, like a hockey puck. Cover each with plastic wrap and chill in the refrigerator while you prepare the filling.

● To prepare the filling, mix together the potatoes, onion, and sirloin in a large bowl. Mix in the salt and pepper.

● Position a rack in the center of the oven and preheat to 400°F.

On a well-floured surface, roll out one circle of dough into a 10-inch circle. Spread half of the filling over half of the circle, leaving a 1-inch border. Dot with 1 tablespoon of the butter. Fold the circle in half, forming a half-moon shape, flatten gently, and roll up, leaving a ½-inch border to seal tightly. Cut a few small vents in the top of the pastry with the tip of a sharp knife. Gently transfer to a lightly buttered 12-inch cast iron skillet. Repeat with the second circle of dough, the remaining tablespoon of butter, and the rest of the filling. Carefully place the second pasty in the skillet so that the two form a full circle. Place the skillet in the oven and bake for 50 minutes. Cut in half and transfer carefully to dinner plates. Serve warm with ketchup for dipping.

CLASSIC GRILLED REUBEN

Reubens are named after Arthur Reuben, who created this delicious sandwich in his New York delicatessen in 1941. We bet he didn't realize it would still be such a hit today. New York's Katz Deli is still our favorite place to get a true Reuben. Larry Kramis enjoys his with a little horseradish cream. Sometimes we slice this sandwich into eighths and serve it as an appetizer. A crispy kosher pickle makes a perfect finishing touch.

• • ● • •

MAKES 1 SANDWICH

> 2 slices rye or dill rye bread
> 2 teaspoons butter, at room temperature
> 2 tablespoons Russian or Thousand Island dressing
> 4 to 5 ounces pastrami or corned beef
> 2 ounces sauerkraut or coleslaw
> 2 slices Swiss cheese

● Lightly butter one side of each slice of bread. (The buttered sides are the outside of the sandwich.) On the other side of each slice (the inside), spread 1 tablespoon Russian dressing. On the bottom half, layer, in order, the pastrami, the sauerkraut, and the cheese. Top with the other slice of bread, butter side up.

● Heat a cast iron skillet or griddle over medium heat. Allow the pan to heat for 2 minutes. Place the sandwich in the pan and press down on it with a lid from another pot or with another iron skillet. Cook until golden brown. Flip with a spatula (use your hand to hold the sandwich together while flipping), and grill the other side until golden. Cut in half and serve.

SIDES

Rosemary Roasted Potatoes
Sweet Potato Soufflé
Rösti Potatoes
Potato Pancakes
Skillet-Roasted Asparagus
Roasted Root Vegetables
Moist Cornbread
Herbed Skillet Bread
Fennel-Ricotta Skillet Bread
Sautéed Swiss Chard with Caramelized Onions
Cornbread Pudding
Savory Tarte Tatin
Ginger-Glazed Carrots
Skillet-Roasted Tomatoes with Toasted Crumbs
Warm Swiss Chard Bread Salad
Best Baked Beans
Caramelized Shallots
Elsie's Zucchini Pancakes with Sour Cream Sauce

101

The cast iron skillet is such a perfect match for so many side dishes, it was hard to narrow down our list: Potatoes, potatoes, potatoes! The skillet works magic on them. The Moist Cornbread, Herbed Skillet Bread, and Fennel-Ricotta Skillet Bread are naturals for cast iron. They come out light and fluffy with crispy, golden crusts. The caramelization that takes place with the Caramelized Shallots and the Ginger-Glazed Carrots makes them as good as candy.

These are the side dishes we most often prepare. Once you get a feeling for how the cast iron skillet browns and crisps vegetables and brings out their flavors, you can experiment with all kinds of vegetables. Choose whatever is in season and then sauté or caramelize it in your cast iron skillet, exploring new flavors along the way.

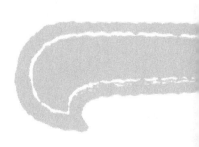

ROSEMARY ROASTED POTATOES

Crisp on the outside, creamy and soft on the inside, these potatoes are perfect alongside roast chicken.

• • ● • •

MAKES 4 SERVINGS

2½ pounds small Yukon Gold potatoes, scrubbed (but not peeled)
¼ cup extra virgin olive oil
1 tablespoon chopped fresh rosemary
Sea salt
Freshly ground black pepper

● Position a rack in the center of the oven and preheat to 400°F.

● Cut each potato into 6 wedges. Toss with the olive oil and rosemary, coating them completely. Season with salt and pepper. Place in a 10- or 12-inch cast iron skillet, and put the skillet in the oven. Roast until crisp and golden, 30 to 40 minutes.

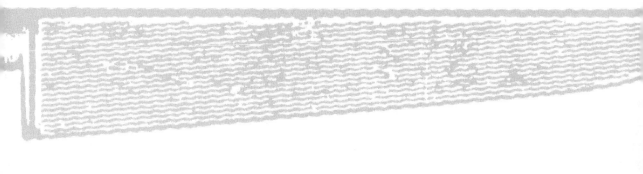

SWEET POTATO SOUFFLÉ

Sweet potatoes are simply underutilized. They tend to be relegated to Thanks-giving, and instead they should be included in our weekly repertoire. They are sweet, golden, and healthy.

• • • • •

MAKES 6 TO 8 SERVINGS

8 medium sweet potatoes or yams (about 4 pounds)
1 teaspoon salt
5 tablespoons salted butter, at room temperature
½ cup half-and-half
¼ cup apple cider
3 tablespoons light brown sugar
½ teaspoon ground cinnamon
1 teaspoon grated orange zest
3 tablespoons chilled salted butter, cut into small pieces

● Position a rack in the center of the oven and preheat to 350°F.

● Put the sweet potatoes in a large stockpot, cover with cold water, and add the salt. Bring to a boil over high heat. Reduce the heat to medium and cook until soft when pierced, 30 to 40 minutes. Drain and allow to cool.

● Peel the sweet potatoes and place in a large bowl. Mash to a coarse consistency with a potato ricer or masher. Add the 5 tablespoons room-temperature butter, half-and-half, apple cider, brown sugar, cinnamon, and orange zest. Beat with an electric mixer on medium speed until fluffy, about 2 minutes.

● Transfer to a buttered 10- or 12-inch cast iron skillet. Dot the potatoes with the chilled butter pieces and bake in the oven until the top is golden brown, about 30 minutes. For a perfect golden crust on top, broil for the last 5 minutes.

Note: **If prepared ahead of time, top with the butter pieces just before reheating.**

RÖSTI POTATOES

This crisp potato pancake is a Kramis family tradition. We have strong family ties to Switzerland and have been enriched by family exchanges over the years. Our most memorable meals always include rösti. For a light supper, add the grated cheese and serve with a green salad.

• • • • •

MAKES 6 SERVINGS

2 pounds russet potatoes, scrubbed and unpeeled
4 tablespoons vegetable oil, divided
4 tablespoons (½ stick) butter, divided
Salt and freshly ground black pepper
½ cup grated Gruyère cheese

Bring a large pot of lightly salted water to a boil over high heat. Add the potatoes and cook for 10 minutes. Drain. Cool to room temperature.

Peel the potatoes and coarsely grate them (a food processor fitted with a medium-sized grater does the quickest work).

Heat 2 tablespoons of the oil and 2 tablespoons of the butter in a 10-inch cast iron skillet over medium heat. Add the grated potatoes and brown until a crisp, golden crust forms, about 10 minutes, gently pressing down on the potatoes with a spatula occasionally. Season with salt and pepper.

Invert the potatoes by placing a plate face down on top of the skillet. Using oven mitts, grasp the skillet and plate firmly with 2 hands and carefully turn the potatoes onto the plate. Add the remaining 2 tablespoons butter and oil to the skillet, let the butter melt, and then return the rösti to the skillet with the crisp side up; cook for 10 minutes longer. Transfer to a serving platter and season again with salt and pepper. Scatter the grated Gruyère cheese over the top and serve hot.

POTATO PANCAKES

So easy! So good! Serve these pancakes as an appetizer by making them smaller and topping them with sour cream and caviar. The secret to success lies in not making them too thick—¼ inch thick is the best. The cast iron skillet browns the pancake and forms a crisp crust on the outside.

• • ● • •

MAKES 6 SERVINGS

1 egg, beaten
2 tablespoons all-purpose flour
1 teaspoon baking powder
1 russet potato, peeled and grated
¼ yellow onion, grated
2 tablespoons canola oil

• • ● • •

Sour cream, for garnish
Chopped chives, for garnish

● In a medium bowl, whisk together the egg, flour, and baking powder.

● Peel and grate the potato on the medium-sized holes of a box grater. Place in a colander and rinse lightly with cold water. Press with paper towels to blot excess moisture. Grate the onion. Add the grated potatoes and onions to the egg mixture and mix.

● Heat the oil over medium heat in a 12-inch cast iron skillet. Scoop ⅓ cup of the potato mixture into the pan. Flatten with a spatula to a thickness of ¼ inch. Cook until golden, 3 minutes on each side. You will have to cook them in 2 batches. Add a little more oil if necessary. Garnish with sour cream and chives.

SKILLET-ROASTED ASPARAGUS

Northwest asparagus appears in our farmers' markets in late March. This simple and delicious preparation captures the sweetness of the asparagus and offers a tasty alternative to the customary steaming. It's a perfect accompaniment to the first halibut of the season.

• • ● • •

MAKES 4 SERVINGS

> 1 pound fresh asparagus spears, ½ inch thick
> 3 tablespoons extra virgin olive oil
> Sea salt and freshly ground black pepper

● Position a rack in the center of the oven and preheat to 400°F.

● Trim off the tough ends of the asparagus. Place the spears in a 10- or 12-inch cast iron skillet. Pour the olive oil over the spears and, with your hands, turn the asparagus until it is evenly coated with oil. Bake until tender, 12 to 15 minutes. Sprinkle with salt and pepper and serve in the warm skillet.

ROASTED ROOT VEGETABLES

The saltiness of the bacon really brings out the flavors of the vegetables. Serve these with salmon, roast chicken, or pork roast. Other than requiring a little chopping, this is an easy way to enjoy a variety of vegetables.

• • ● • •

MAKES 6 SERVINGS

3 strips bacon
1 medium yellow onion, chopped
1 celery root, peeled, root end removed, and cut into small cubes
1 parsnip, peeled, root end removed, and cut into small wedges
1 rutabaga, peeled, root end removed, and cut into small wedges
1 large golden beet, peeled, root end removed, and cut into small
   wedges
$\frac{1}{2}$ cup water
Salt and freshly ground black pepper

• • ● • •

1 teaspoon chopped fresh flat-leaf parsley, for serving

● Place the bacon in a 10- or 12-inch cast iron skillet and cook, stirring occasionally, over medium heat until golden brown, about 5 minutes. Transfer to paper towels, leaving the fat in the pan.

● With the skillet over medium heat, add the onions and cook, stirring occasionally, until lightly browned, about 5 minutes. Add the celery root, parsnips, rutabagas, and beets and toss. Add the water, cover, and cook until tender when poked with a knife, about 10 minutes more. (They should still be a bit firm.) Uncover and cook, tossing occasionally, until lightly browned, about 5 minutes more. Season with salt and pepper, crumble the reserved bacon over the top, sprinkle with parsley, and serve.

MOIST CORNBREAD

We use this cornbread as the base for our Cornbread Pudding (see page 115) because it doesn't crumble; it's also terrific on its own, served with melted butter and honey. For variety, try adding fresh herbs or ²/₃ cup grated dry Jack, pepper Jack, or sharp cheddar cheese to the batter. We like Bob's Red Mill cornmeal—see Resources, page 158, for information.

• • ● • •

MAKES 8 SERVINGS

1 cup finely ground yellow cornmeal
1 cup all-purpose flour
1½ teaspoons baking powder
½ teaspoon baking soda
2 tablespoons granulated sugar
½ teaspoon salt
½ teaspoon chili powder
2 large eggs
½ cup sour cream
1 cup half-and-half
6 tablespoons (¾ stick) butter, melted
²/₃ cup fresh or frozen corn, thawed and drained if frozen

● Position a rack in the center of the oven and preheat to 400°F.

● Generously butter the sides and bottom of an 8- or 10-inch skillet. In a large bowl, whisk together the cornmeal, flour, baking powder, baking soda, sugar, salt, and chili powder. In a medium bowl, whisk together the eggs, sour cream, half-and-half, 4 tablespoons of the melted butter (allow it to cool slightly before adding), and corn. Add the egg mixture to the cornmeal mixture and stir until just combined. Do not overmix.

● Heat the skillet over medium heat. Pour the cornmeal batter into the skillet, jiggling the skillet slightly to level out the batter.

● Bake in the oven for 10 minutes. Remove the skillet from the oven and pour the remaining 2 tablespoons of melted butter over the top. Return to the oven and continue baking until golden brown and a toothpick inserted in the center comes out clean, about 10 minutes more. Cool. Cut into wedges and serve.

HERBED SKILLET BREAD

The aroma of freshly baked bread and rosemary fills your kitchen when this is in the oven. The cast iron skillet acts like a wood-burning oven and makes a wonderful crisp crust. This easy bread is excellent with roast chicken and ribs.

• • • • •

MAKES 8 SERVINGS

1 tablespoon sugar
1 cup warm water (105°F), divided
1 package active dry yeast
2¼ cups all-purpose flour, plus more as needed
2 teaspoons sea salt, divided
¼ cup plus 2 tablespoons olive oil, divided, plus more for drizzling
2 cloves garlic, thinly sliced
2 sprigs fresh rosemary, chopped

• In a large bowl, dissolve the sugar in ½ cup of the warm water. Sprinkle the yeast on top and let it sit for 5 minutes. Add the remaining ½ cup water, the flour, ½ teaspoon of the salt, and ¼ cup of the olive oil. Stir with a wooden spoon until well blended and the mixture forms a soft dough.

• Turn the dough out onto a well-floured board and knead until smooth, about 10 minutes. Add additional flour as necessary to prevent the dough from sticking.

• Form the dough into a ball and place in a large, lightly oiled bowl. Turn to coat with the oil. Seal the bowl tightly with plastic wrap and let the dough rise for 45 minutes.

• Coat the bottom and sides of a 10-inch skillet with 1 tablespoon olive oil. Place the dough in the skillet and press it evenly into the bottom of the pan. With a sharp knife, score the top lightly in a crisscross pattern. Brush with the remaining 1 tablespoon olive oil and sprinkle the garlic and rosemary over the top. Sprinkle with the remaining 1½ teaspoons sea salt. Let rise for 20 minutes.

* While the bread is rising, position a rack in the center of the oven and preheat oven to 400°F.

* Place the skillet in the hot oven and bake for 20 to 25 minutes, until crust is a light golden color. Remove from the pan right away and place on a wire rack to retain the crisp crust. Drizzle a little olive oil over the top, slice into wedges, and serve warm.

FENNEL-RICOTTA SKILLET BREAD

Our good friend David Moll's cooking specialty is bread baking. This is one of his favorite breads to make. The ricotta cheese makes it very moist, and no kneading is required. Although the bread is simple to prepare, you will need to allow time for two separate risings, each taking an hour, so plan to make your bread on a relaxing day at home.

• • ● • •

MAKES 8 SERVINGS

1 package active dry yeast
¼ cup warm water (105°F)
1 cup ricotta cheese, warmed to 100°F to 110°F in a microwave oven
1 tablespoon butter
2 tablespoons sugar
1 teaspoon salt
¼ teaspoon baking soda
2 teaspoons fennel seeds
1 egg
2 cups all-purpose flour
Butter, at room temperature, for topping
Sea salt, for topping

● In a small bowl, dissolve the yeast in the warm water for 5 minutes.

● In a large bowl, mix together the warm ricotta cheese, butter, sugar, salt, baking soda, fennel seeds, and egg. Add the yeast mixture. Gradually add all the flour, ½ cup at a time, mixing well after each addition. The batter will be moist and slightly sticky. Remove from the bowl and form into a soft ball on a lightly floured surface.

● Rinse the bowl the dough was in, and then butter the bottom and halfway up the sides. Place the dough in the bowl and cover tightly with plastic wrap. Let rise for 1 hour.

● Push the dough down with the palm of your hand. Shape it evenly into a round, flat circle in a well-buttered 8-inch cast iron skillet. The dough should be touching the sides of the skillet. Cover with plastic wrap and let rise for 1 hour.

● While the bread is rising, position a rack in the center of the oven and preheat to 350°F.

● Remove the plastic wrap, place the skillet in the oven, and bake until golden brown, 35 to 40 minutes. Remove from the oven, brush the top of the bread with soft butter, and sprinkle with sea salt. Then remove from the pan and cool on a baking rack. Cut into wedges and serve.

SAUTÉED SWISS CHARD WITH CARAMELIZED ONIONS

The cast iron skillet works wonders with sautéed greens. It absorbs any excess liquid, leaving the greens tender but not mushy. Rich in flavor, this is an excellent accompaniment to pork, lamb, or chicken. We also like to sauté cooked cannellini beans and toss them in with the onions at the end.

• • ● • •

MAKES 6 SERVINGS

> 3 tablespoons salted butter, divided
> 1 sweet yellow onion, quartered and thinly sliced
> 1 teaspoon sugar
> Salt
> 2 heads Swiss chard, rinsed, dried, and cut into 2-inch strips (stems removed)
> 4 tablespoons orange juice, divided
> 4 tablespoons apple cider, divided
> ¼ teaspoon freshly grated nutmeg, divided
> Freshly ground black pepper

● Melt 1 tablespoon of the butter in a 10- or 12-inch cast iron skillet over medium heat. Add the onions and cook, stirring occasionally, for about 5 minutes. Add the sugar and a pinch of salt and continue cooking until caramelized, 5 to 10 minutes longer. Transfer to a plate.

● Working in 2 batches, add 1 tablespoon of the butter to the skillet and half of the Swiss chard. Stir in 2 tablespoons orange juice, 2 tablespoons apple cider, and ⅛ teaspoon nutmeg. Cook until the liquid starts to evaporate, about 10 minutes. Transfer to a bowl and cover with foil. (You can place the bowl in a 250°F oven to keep warm.) Repeat with the second batch of chard and the remaining butter, orange juice, cider, and nutmeg.

● Add the second batch of chard to the first batch. Add the cooked onions, season with salt and pepper, and toss to mix. Serve immediately.

THE
CAST IRON
SKILLET
COOKBOOK

CORNBREAD PUDDING

Tom Douglas, chef and owner of several of Seattle's top restaurants, inspired this savory pudding. We pair it with barbecued ribs or any slow-cooked meat or salmon. The cornbread stays moist on the inside, crispy and golden on the outside.

• • • • •

MAKES 6 SERVINGS

4½ cups cubed Moist Cornbread (see page 109) or other cornbread
(see note)
1 tablespoon unsalted butter
1 cup thinly sliced yellow onions (about ½ large onion)
¾ cup grated dry Jack cheese, cheddar, or Cougar Gold cheddar (see
Resources, page 158)
2 teaspoons chopped fresh flat-leaf parsley
½ teaspoon chopped fresh rosemary
½ teaspoon chopped fresh thyme leaves
2 cups heavy cream
3 large eggs
1 teaspoon kosher salt
½ teaspoon freshly ground black pepper

◦ Position a rack in the center of the oven and preheat to 350°F.

◦ Put the cubed cornbread in a buttered 10- or 12-inch cast iron skillet. Set aside. Heat the butter in another skillet over low heat, add the onions, and cook very slowly, stirring occasionally, until soft and golden brown, at least 20 minutes. Remove from the heat. Scatter the onions, cheese, parsley, rosemary, and thyme over the cornbread cubes. Whisk the heavy cream and eggs with the salt and pepper in a mixing bowl and pour over the cornbread cubes. Let sit for 10 minutes to allow the cornbread to absorb some of the custard. Bake until set and golden, about 40 minutes. Serve hot.

Note: **To save time, you can substitute cornbread made from a mix for our Moist Cornbread. Just be sure to let the cornbread cool completely before cutting it into cubes. For a more custard-like version of the pudding, increase the heavy cream to 3 cups, and use 4 eggs.**

SAVORY TARTE TATIN
(Upside-Down Vegetable Tart)

This is an adaptation of a classic French dessert made with apples, tarte Tatin. In this savory version, the vegetables caramelize beautifully and the crust comes out light and flaky in the iron skillet. This makes a flavorful vegetarian main dish. We also love using onions and wild mushrooms instead of root vegetables.

• • • • •

MAKES 8 SERVINGS

Pastry
1¼ cups all-purpose flour

¼ teaspoon salt

6 tablespoons (¾ stick) chilled unsalted butter, cut into small pieces

2 tablespoons chilled vegetable shortening

5 tablespoons ice-cold water

Filling
1 large carrot, peeled, cut into thirds, and then quartered

1 large turnip, peeled, root end removed, cut in half, and then cut into ½-inch wedges

1 parsnip, peeled, root end removed, and cut into 1-inch wedges

1 teaspoon salt

1 large rutabaga, peeled, root end removed, cut in half, and cut into ½-inch wedges

1 sweet yellow onion, root end trimmed but still attached, cut into 1½-inch wedges

2 tablespoons olive oil

1 teaspoon chopped fresh rosemary

1 teaspoon fresh thyme leaves

¼ teaspoon freshly grated nutmeg

Salt and freshly ground black pepper

¼ cup (½ stick) butter, cut into small pieces

1 teaspoon Pernod (optional)

2 teaspoons sugar

Egg Wash for Crust
1 egg
1 tablespoon water

* To prepare the crust, place the flour and salt in a large bowl or in a food processor. Mix, then add the butter and shortening. Cut in with a pastry blender or pulse in the processor until the mixture has the consistency of small peas. Add the water, 1 tablespoon at a time, and mix gently with your hand, or pulse quickly just until the dough sticks together and you can form it into a ball. Do not knead the dough. Form the dough into a thick disk, wrap in plastic wrap, and chill in the refrigerator for 30 minutes.

* Position a rack in the center of the oven and preheat to 400°F.

* To prepare the filling, place the carrots, turnips, and parsnips in a 4-quart saucepan. Add enough water to cover the vegetables. Add the salt and bring to a boil over medium-high heat. Reduce the heat to medium and maintain a low boil. Add the rutabagas and cook for 5 minutes. Drain.

* Transfer the partially cooked vegetables and the onion to a large bowl. Add the olive oil, rosemary, thyme, and nutmeg, stirring gently until everything is thoroughly coated. Season to taste with salt and pepper.

* Scatter the butter pieces in a 10- or 12-inch cast iron skillet. Place over low heat and cook until the butter melts. Stir in the Pernod, if using, and the sugar. Add the vegetables to the skillet and increase the heat to medium-high. Do not stir the vegetables, but gently move them around to fill in any empty gaps. Occasionally press down on them gently with a spatula while they brown, about 5 minutes. Remove from heat.

* Roll out the pastry dough into a 10- to 12-inch circle. Lay the dough on top of the vegetables, tucking in any excess dough around the edges. Beat the egg and water together until combined, and lightly brush the top of the crust. Make four 1-inch cuts in the top to vent steam. Place the skillet in the oven and bake for 20 to 25 minutes. Remove from the oven and let cool for 5 minutes.

* Place a large plate upside down on top of the skillet. Protecting both hands with oven mitts, grasp the skillet and the plate firmly with both hands, pressing the plate tightly onto the skillet. Invert the tart onto the plate. Slice into wedges and serve.

GINGER-GLAZED CARROTS

These carrots are a perfect example of why the cast iron skillet is so important in your kitchen. The tender carrots caramelize with the butter, ginger, and sugar, bringing out their sweetness.

• • ● • •

MAKES 4 SERVINGS

1½ pounds carrots, peeled and cut into ½-inch slices or into a
   diagonal or V-cut
¾ cup water
¼ cup (½ stick) salted butter
1-inch piece fresh ginger, peeled and thinly sliced
2 tablespoons sugar

• • ● • •

Sea salt
1 tablespoon chopped fresh parsley, for garnish

● Place the carrots, water, butter, ginger, and sugar in a 10-inch cast iron skillet. Bring to a boil over medium-high heat, reduce the heat to medium-low, simmer and cook for 10 minutes, stirring occasionally until the carrots are tender and a buttery sauce has developed. Season with sea salt, garnish with parsley, and serve immediately.

SKILLET-ROASTED TOMATOES
WITH TOASTED CRUMBS

This is a good way to serve tomatoes in the winter months, when they are firm and not as flavorful as the late-summer sweet, vine-ripened tomatoes. The acidity of the tomatoes causes them to absorb a little of the healthy iron from the pan.

• • • • •

MAKES 8 SERVINGS

4 medium-sized tomatoes
2 cups fresh white bread crumbs
¼ cup extra virgin olive oil
¼ cup finely chopped fresh parsley
1 teaspoon dried herbes de Provence
Salt and freshly ground black pepper

● Position a rack in the center of the oven and preheat to 375°F.

● Cut the tomatoes in half crosswise. Remove the stem ends. Place cut side up in a 10- or 12-inch cast iron skillet.

● In a medium-sized bowl, mix the bread crumbs, olive oil, parsley, and herbes de Provence. Evenly top each of the tomato halves with the bread crumb mixture. Season with salt and pepper.

● Place the skillet in the oven and bake until the tomatoes begin to soften and the bread crumbs turn golden brown, about 15 minutes. Serve warm.

WARM SWISS CHARD BREAD SALAD

This is a starch and a vegetable, all in one dish. The crisp bread cubes and warm wilted greens complement each other well.

• • ● • •

MAKES 8 TO 10 SERVINGS

Croutons
8 ounces soft rustic bread, cut into 1-inch cubes (4 cups)
¼ cup extra virgin olive oil

Salad
2 tablespoons extra virgin olive oil
1 yellow onion, chopped
3 large leeks, white and light green parts only, rinsed well and chopped
6 cloves garlic, minced
1 pound Swiss chard, de-ribbed and cut into 2-inch pieces
1½ cups (one 14.5-ounce can) cooked Great Northern beans or cannellini beans
1 cup chicken stock
Juice of 1 lemon
½ teaspoon freshly grated nutmeg
Salt and freshly ground black pepper
½ cup half-and-half
2 cups (8 ounces) grated Swiss or Gruyère cheese

● To prepare the croutons, position a rack at the top of the oven and preheat the broiler. Toss the bread cubes with the olive oil in a large bowl. Spread the bread cubes in an even layer on a baking sheet and broil until golden brown, 3 to 5 minutes. Watch them carefully because they can easily burn. Flip the bread cubes over and return the baking sheet to the oven for 3 minutes more to brown the other side. Remove from the oven and set aside.

● To prepare the salad, position a rack in the center of the oven and preheat to 350°F.

● Heat the olive oil in a 10- or 12-inch cast iron skillet over medium heat. Add the onions, leeks, and garlic. Cook, stirring occasionally, until softened, about 5 minutes. Stir in the Swiss chard, cover, and cook for 15 minutes. Add the beans and toss gently. Stir in the chicken stock, lemon juice, nutmeg, and salt and pepper to taste. (Go slightly heavier on the salt than the pepper.) Bring to a low boil. Spread the croutons on top, gently pressing them down into the mixture with a spatula. Pour the half-and-half over the croutons. Sprinkle the grated cheese evenly over the top of the croutons.

● Cover the skillet with foil and bake in the oven for 25 minutes. Remove the foil, turn on the broiler, and broil until the cheese is bubbly and golden brown, about 5 minutes more. Remove from the oven and let cool for 5 minutes before serving.

BEST BAKED BEANS

There's nothing like making your own baked beans. These beans have a wonderful blend of spices, without the high sodium content of canned beans. Although they take several hours to cook, you can just leave them unattended and let them slow-cook.

• • ● • •

MAKES 12 SERVINGS

8 cups cold water
2¾ cups (1 pound) dried Great Northern beans
4 strips bacon
½ yellow onion, diced
1 cup beer, preferably pale ale
2 cups water
½ cup molasses
¼ cup maple syrup
1 tablespoon Worcestershire sauce
2 tablespoons light brown sugar
2 teaspoons dry mustard
1 teaspoon paprika
2 teaspoons salt

● In a large stockpot, bring the cold water to a boil over high heat. Add the beans to the boiling water and cook for 2 minutes. Remove from the heat, cover, and let soak for 1 hour. Drain in a colander and rinse the beans.

● Heat a 10- or 12-inch cast iron skillet over medium heat. Add the bacon and cook until golden, turning once. Transfer the bacon to a paper towel. Pour off all but 3 tablespoons of the bacon fat.

● Return the skillet to medium heat. Add the onion and cook, stirring occasionally and scraping up the browned bits from the bacon, until golden brown. Add the beans, beer, water, molasses, maple syrup, Worcestershire sauce, brown sugar, dry mustard, and paprika. Coarsely chop the bacon and add it to the skillet. Reduce the heat to medium-low (or place the skillet in a 250°F oven) and cook, covered, for 3 hours. Add water as needed to keep the beans covered. During the last half hour of cooking, remove the lid and don't add any additional water to the beans. When the beans are done, stir in the salt just before serving.

CARAMELIZED SHALLOTS

The cast iron skillet caramelizes the shallots, leaving them soft and sweet. We love these shallots as a side dish for chicken and turkey. They also pair well with green beans or braised carrots.

• • • • •

MAKES 6 TO 8 SERVINGS

10 to 12 whole shallot cloves (1 shallot usually has 2 cloves)
¼ cup extra virgin olive oil
¼ cup balsamic vinegar
½ teaspoon salt
3 tablespoons brown sugar

• Position a rack in the center of the oven and preheat to 400°F.

• Peel the shallots. Trim off the rough part of the root, but leave the soft part of the root attached. Cut large shallot cloves into quarters and smaller cloves in half. Place in a medium-sized bowl. Add the olive oil, vinegar, salt, and brown sugar. Toss to coat.

• Place in a 10- or 12-inch cast iron skillet and cover with foil. Bake for 20 minutes. Remove the foil, gently toss the shallots, and continue baking until golden and soft, another 20 minutes.

ELSIE'S ZUCCHINI PANCAKES WITH SOUR CREAM SAUCE

At the end of summer, if you're growing zucchini in your garden, you need recipes to use them all. (They seem to appear overnight.) We like to serve these zucchini pancakes with grilled chicken or fish.

• • • • •

MAKES 6 SERVINGS

Sour Cream Sauce

¾ cup sour cream
2 tablespoons finely chopped green onion, both green and white parts
¼ cup dry white wine
1 tablespoon fresh lemon juice

Zucchini Pancakes

3 cups grated zucchini (about 4 medium-sized zucchini)
2 tablespoons all-purpose flour
2 tablespoons freshly grated Parmesan cheese
¼ cup finely chopped green onion, white and green parts (about 3 onions)
3 large eggs, beaten
1 tablespoon fresh lemon juice
1 tablespoon canola oil, plus more as needed

• • • • •

Finely chopped chives, for garnish

● To prepare the Sour Cream Sauce, mix together the sour cream, green onion, wine, and lemon juice in a small saucepan and cook over medium heat just until warm. Reduce the heat to low while you prepare the pancakes.

● Preheat the oven to 250°F and place a platter in the oven to warm.

● To prepare the pancakes, place the grated zucchini between 2 layers of paper towels and press lightly to remove some of the moisture. Transfer to a large bowl. Add the flour and mix to coat. Add the Parmesan cheese, green onions, eggs, and lemon juice and mix well.

• Heat 1 tablespoon canola oil in a 10- or 12-inch cast iron skillet over medium heat. Drop ⅓ cup pancake batter into the skillet for each pancake and cook, turning once, until golden brown on both sides, 2 to 3 minutes. Transfer to the warm platter in the oven and repeat until you have used all the batter, adding more oil to the skillet as needed.

• To serve, pour a little of the warm Sour Cream Sauce over the pancakes and garnish with chopped chives.

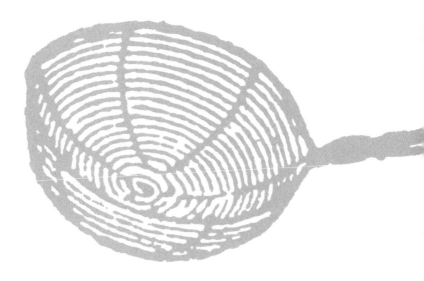

OUTDOOR COOKERY

Skillet-Roasted Clams with Garlic and Parsley
Seafood Bake
Cast Iron Chili
Pan-Fried Trout
Arroz con Pollo

127

ooking outdoors doesn't have to be a rugged experience. Whether we are camping in the woods or grilling on the backyard barbecue, we like to keep it simple. Summertime family gatherings at the beach are the perfect setting for the one-pot Seafood Bake cooked on a grate over a fire pit. The Arroz Con Pollo and Cast Iron Chili are also one-pot meals that are sure to satisfy a hungry family after a day spent outdoors. When you are planning a camping trip, just prepare your ingredients ahead and store them in resealable plastic bags. When you're ready to cook, dinner will come together quickly.

Cast iron Dutch ovens and skillets—and all of these recipes—work equally well on outdoor grills or on a grate over an open fire. The best way to test the heat of an open fire is with your hand. Hold it about 3 inches above the fire, and time how long you can keep it there before you are forced to pull it away.

• 1 to 2 seconds: high heat. Best for searing meat and grilling shrimp.

• 3 to 5 seconds: medium heat. Best for most types of fish.

• 6 to 7 seconds: low heat. Perfect for grilling vegetables and slow-cooking dishes.

An outdoor meal wouldn't be complete without s'mores, so don't forget to pack the graham crackers, marshmallows, and chocolate bars along with your cast iron skillet.

SKILLET-ROASTED CLAMS WITH GARLIC AND PARSLEY

We love to dig clams at our family beach house in South Puget Sound. We can gather a large bucket of small Manila clams in 15 minutes and enjoy them later for dinner.

• • ● • •

MAKES 4 SERVINGS

¼ cup (½ stick) butter
2 cloves garlic, minced
1 to 2 teaspoons crushed red pepper flakes
¼ cup dry white wine
¼ cup water
Juice of 1 lemon
4 pounds small steamer clams, soaked and rinsed

• • ● • •

2 tablespoons chopped fresh parsley, for garnish
Crusty French bread, for serving

● Place the butter, garlic, and red pepper flakes in a cast iron Dutch oven over medium heat (or on a grate over a medium-heat fire). Melt the butter and simmer for 2 minutes. Add the wine, water, lemon juice, and clams. Stir to coat the clams. Cover and cook until all of the clams have opened, about 5 minutes. Sprinkle the parsley over the top and serve in shallow bowls with crusty French bread for dipping.

SEAFOOD BAKE

An incredible one-pot meal! Feel free to toss in whatever kind of seafood is fresh and available.

• • ● • •

MAKES 6 SERVINGS

3 tablespoons extra virgin olive oil
1 pound kielbasa (Polish sausage), cut into 1-inch pieces
1 fresh fennel bulb, trimmed, halved lengthwise, and thinly sliced crosswise
2 teaspoons fresh thyme
2 cloves garlic, finely chopped
1 medium yellow onion, coarsely chopped
1 cup dry white wine
1½ cups clam juice
1 can (14.5 ounces) chopped tomatoes, drained
2 teaspoons Old Bay seasoning
½ teaspoon crushed red pepper flakes
3 ears corn, husked and snapped in half
Grated zest of ½ lemon
10 small red potatoes (about 1 pound), cooked
2 pounds mussels, scrubbed and debearded
2 pounds clams, rinsed
2 crabs (2 pounds each), cooked, cleaned, top shell removed, and body cut into quarters, keeping legs attached
Juice of 1 lemon
¼ cup coarsely chopped fresh parsley
Salt and freshly ground black pepper

• • ● • •

Lemon wedges, for garnish
Crusty loaf of bread, for serving

● Heat a 6- to 8-quart Dutch oven over the stove top or open fire using medium-high heat (using the heat method on page 128).

**THE
CAST IRON
SKILLET
COOKBOOK**

• Combine the olive oil, kielbasa, fennel, thyme, garlic, and onions in your Dutch oven and cook for 10 minutes, stirring occasionally. Add the wine, clam juice, tomatoes, Old Bay seasoning, and crushed red pepper flakes, and stir. If cooking over a fire, bring to a boil directly over a medium-high-heat fire. Then move the Dutch oven off to the side for indirect heat. Cover and cook for 10 minutes.

• Add the corn and lemon zest and cook for 5 minutes. Add the cooked potatoes, mussels, clams, and crabs; cover and cook until the mussels have opened, 5 minutes more. Squeeze the lemon juice over the top, sprinkle with parsley, and season with salt and pepper. Serve in large individual bowls with lemon wedges and a crusty loaf of bread.

CAST IRON CHILI

After skiing or just relaxing on a crisp, cool day, nothing's better than a hot pot of chili on the stove. This is a simple, quick version of a longtime favorite. It works equally well over a campfire or on your kitchen stove. Top with cheddar cheese and sour cream and serve with a basket of Moist Cornbread (see page 109).

• • ● • •

MAKES 6 SERVINGS

2 tablespoons vegetable oil
1 cup chopped yellow onion
1 pound lean ground beef
¾ cup chopped green bell pepper
1 tablespoon chili powder
2 cans (15.25 ounces each) kidney beans, drained and rinsed
1 teaspoon crushed red pepper flakes
1 can (28 ounces) diced tomatoes, with their juice
1 cup canned crushed tomatoes

• • • • •

Sour cream, for serving
Chopped green onions, for serving
Grated cheddar cheese, for serving

● Heat the oil in a cast iron Dutch oven over medium heat on a grill or on a grate over a medium-heat fire (see page 128). Add the onions and cook, stirring often, for 5 minutes. Add the ground beef, stirring to crumble the meat while it browns. After the meat browns, add the green peppers and cook for 2 minutes more. Stir in the chili powder, kidney beans, and chile flakes. Add the tomatoes with their juice and the tomato purée. Stir well and simmer for 15 minutes. Serve in bowls, topped with sour cream, chopped green onions, and grated cheddar cheese.

PAN-FRIED TROUT

Bring your cast iron skillet on your next fishing trip, and ideally you will catch something you can cook in it. Fresh trout will never taste better. Trout is very easy to cook and eat because it has just one big bone that can quickly be removed. Relax by the river, take in the view, and enjoy the wonderful flavors of your fresh catch. Potato salad makes a good accompaniment.

• • • • •

MAKES 2 SERVINGS

    1 large or 2 small fresh trout, cleaned and filleted
    1 teaspoon salt, plus more for seasoning fish
    ½ teaspoon freshly ground black pepper, plus more for seasoning fish
    ¼ cup flour
    6 tablespoons (¾ stick) butter, divided
    Juice of 1 lemon
    1 tablespoon capers

Season the trout fillets with salt and pepper. Mix together the flour, 1 teaspoon salt, and ½ teaspoon pepper in a shallow dish. Lightly coat the fish with the flour mixture.

Heat 3 tablespoons of the butter in a 10- or 12-inch cast iron skillet over medium-high heat on a grill or on a grate over a medium-heat fire (see page 128). Place the fillets flesh side down in the skillet and cook for 5 minutes. Turn over and cook for another 3 to 5 minutes. Transfer to a plate.

Melt the remaining 3 tablespoons butter in the skillet over medium heat. Stir in the lemon juice and capers. Pour the sauce over the trout and serve.

ARROZ CON POLLO

This classic Mexican one-dish meal is especially wonderful on a camping trip. Simplify your campsite preparation by chopping all the vegetables in advance and premeasuring the spices and rice. Transport everything in resealable plastic bags. Then assemble and cook in your Dutch oven. The rice turns a beautiful golden color from the saffron and paprika. The chicken is juicy, and the peppers add nice flavor.

• • ● • •

MAKES 4 TO 6 SERVINGS

2 tablespoons butter
1 large fryer chicken, cut into 8 pieces (or purchase 2 bone-in skinless breasts, 2 drumsticks, and 2 skinless thighs)
2 large white onions, coarsely chopped
2 bell peppers (1 red, 1 green), coarsely chopped
2 cloves garlic, minced
1½ cans (14.5 ounces each) diced tomatoes, with their juice
2 cups chicken stock
1 teaspoon paprika
Pinch saffron
Salt and freshly ground black pepper
2 cups uncooked long-grain white rice
Juice of 1 lemon

● Melt the butter in a cast iron Dutch oven over a medium-heat fire or over medium heat on a camp stove. Add the chicken and cook, turning occasionally, until lightly browned on all sides. Transfer to a plate.

● Add the onions, peppers, and garlic to the pan and cook, stirring occasionally, for 10 minutes. Stir in the tomatoes, chicken stock, paprika, saffron, salt, and pepper. Cook for 5 minutes. Stir in the rice. Add the chicken to the pan and spoon the sauce over the chicken, submerging it as much as possible. Cook very slowly over a low- to medium-heat fire, or over low heat on a camp stove for approximately 45 minutes. Occasionally, turn the

chicken gently and turn the pot to move the rice, but do not stir. Season to taste with additional salt, pepper, and lemon juice and serve.

Note: **To add extra flavor, remove 2 chorizo sausages from their casings and add the meat to the pan before you brown the chicken. Brown the sausage, transfer to a plate, and reserve. Add the sausage to the vegetable mixture when you add the chicken.**

DESSERTS

Sautéed Bananas in Rum
Warm Pear-Ginger Upside-Down Cake
Tarte Tatin (Upside-Down Apple Tart)
Old-Fashioned Peach Dumplings with Nutmeg Cream
Cardamom-Apricot Financier
Bread Pudding with Grand Marnier Sauce
Apple Cake with Caramel Frosting and Chopped Pecans
Bing Cherry Clafouti
Skillet Baked Apples
Plum Galette
Caramelized Apple and Gingerbread Cake

137

Upside-down cakes, Bread Pudding with Grand Marnier Sauce, Old-Fashioned Peach Dumplings, and Sautéed Bananas in Rum are classic examples of desserts that are perfect for the cast iron skillet because it conducts heat so evenly. Fruit caramelizes beautifully, crusts bake to golden, flaky perfection, and cakes come out light and moist. The Plum Galette and Bing Cherry Clafouti have a rustic feel when served in the hot skillet. Others, such as the Tarte Tatin and the Warm Pear-Ginger Upside-Down Cake are meant to be served right side up on a platter so everyone can see the beautiful caramelization and symmetry of the apples and pears.

SAUTÉED BANANAS IN RUM

Cactus restaurant in Seattle's Madison Park neighborhood is the source of this delicious dessert. Serve in individual dessert dishes and top with vanilla ice cream.

• • • • •

MAKES 4 SERVINGS

¼ cup (½ stick) butter, cut into pieces
½ cup light brown sugar
1 tablespoon Myers dark rum
2 ripe medium-sized bananas, peeled and halved crosswise, then lengthwise

• • • • •

Coconut or Mexican vanilla ice cream, for serving

● Melt the butter in a small saucepan over medium heat. Add the brown sugar and cook, stirring constantly, until the sugar has completely dissolved. Whisk in the rum. Continue whisking until all the ingredients are well combined. Remove from the heat.

● Heat an 8- or 12-inch cast iron skillet over medium-high heat. Place 3 tablespoons of the rum-butter mixture in the skillet. Place the banana quarters flat side down in the skillet and cook until golden, 2 to 3 minutes. Turn over and cook for 2 minutes more. Bring the skillet to the table and serve in bowls with ice cream.

WARM PEAR-GINGER UPSIDE-DOWN CAKE

We love adding cornmeal to baked goods and pancakes. It gives cakes more substance and texture and, when mixed first with hot water, makes them incredibly moist. The hint of ginger in this cake really pulls all the flavors together. Topped with fresh whipped cream or vanilla ice cream, this is the ideal finish to a winter's feast.

• • ● • •

MAKES 8 TO 10 SERVINGS

    8 tablespoons (1 stick) unsalted butter, at room temperature, divided

    ¾ cup sugar, divided

    2 pounds firm but ripe Bartlett or Anjou pears (about 4 pears), peeled, cored, and cut into eighths

    2 tablespoons minced candied ginger

    ¼ teaspoon freshly grated nutmeg

    1 cup all-purpose flour

    2 teaspoons baking powder

    ¼ teaspoon salt

    ⅓ cup medium-ground yellow cornmeal

    ½ cup boiling water

    2 large eggs

    1 teaspoon vanilla extract

    ½ cup whole milk

● Position a rack in the center of the oven and preheat to 350°F.

● Melt 2 tablespoons of the butter in a 10-inch cast iron skillet over medium heat. Add ¼ cup of the sugar, stir just enough to combine, and cook without disturbing until the sugar dissolves and starts to turn golden brown (caramelize), about 5 minutes. Beginning with the outside edge and working your way toward the center in a circular pattern, arrange the pear slices on top of the caramelized sugar. Sprinkle the ginger and nutmeg over the top. Cook until the pears are soft and the caramel starts to thicken, about 5 minutes more. Remove from the heat and set aside.

✽ In a small bowl, whisk together the flour, baking powder, and salt. Place the cornmeal in a large bowl, add the boiling water, and stir to blend. Add the remaining 6 tablespoons butter and the remaining ½ cup sugar to the cornmeal mixture and mix until well blended. (This can be done by hand.) Beat in the eggs and vanilla. Beat in the flour mixture, a little at a time, alternating it with the milk, making sure not to overmix. Pour the batter on top of the pears in the skillet.

✽ Transfer the skillet to the oven and bake until the top starts to brown and the center of the cake feels firm and springs back when pressed, 18 to 20 minutes. Let the cake cool for 5 minutes. Run a knife around the edge to loosen it, and place an inverted plate on top of the skillet. Protecting both hands with oven mitts, flip the cake onto the plate. Replace any fruit that may have stuck to the skillet. Serve warm or at room temperature.

TARTE TATIN

(Upside-Down Apple Tart)

A classic French dessert, tarte Tatin was meant to be cooked in a cast iron skillet. The apples caramelize perfectly and make a beautiful presentation when the tart is inverted.

• • ● • •

Pastry

1 cup all-purpose flour
½ teaspoon salt
1 tablespoon sugar
6 tablespoons (¾ stick) unsalted butter, cut into small pieces
3 tablespoons ice-cold water

Filling

1 cup (2 sticks) unsalted butter, cut into small pieces
1½ cups sugar
8 to 9 apples (Jonagold, Fuji, or Golden Delicious), peeled, cored, and
  halved

• • • • •

Freshly whipped cream or ice cream, for serving

● To prepare the pastry, sift the flour, salt, and sugar into a medium-sized bowl. Rub the butter into the flour mixture with your fingers until it resembles coarse crumbs. Sprinkle the water into the mixture and gently work it into the dough just until the dough holds together. Form into a ball, wrap in plastic wrap, and refrigerate for 30 minutes or overnight.

● To prepare the filling, scatter the butter pieces evenly over the bottom of a 10-inch cast iron skillet. Sprinkle the sugar evenly over the butter, covering the pan bottom. Arrange the apples tightly together in the skillet in a circular pattern, starting at the outside and working toward the center. The apple halves should be on their sides, holding each other up and all facing the same direction. Place 2 halves in the center of the pan. (During cooking the apples will slide down more into the pan.)

• Place the skillet over medium-low heat and cook, uncovered, until the sugar begins to caramelize (turn golden brown), about 35 to 40 minutes. During cooking, spoon some of the caramelized juices over the apples to help caramelize them.

• Position a rack in the center of the oven and preheat to 400°F.

• Remove the pastry dough from the refrigerator and roll out on a lightly floured surface into a 12-inch circle. Drape the pastry dough over the apples, tucking the excess dough into the skillet without disturbing the apples. Place the skillet on a baking sheet in the oven and bake until the pastry is golden brown, 20 to 25 minutes.

• Remove from the oven and let the tart sit for 3 minutes. Find a plate that is slightly larger than the skillet. Place it upside down on top of the skillet. Protecting both hands with oven mitts, grasp the cast iron skillet and the plate firmly with both hands, pressing the plate tightly onto the skillet. Invert the tart onto the plate. Replace any apples that may have stuck to the skillet. Serve with freshly whipped cream or ice cream.

OLD-FASHIONED PEACH DUMPLINGS WITH NUTMEG CREAM

Our good friend Jackie Clark gave us this recipe, and we are very grateful. We look for medium-sized, tree-ripened peaches to make our Old-Fashioned Peach Dumplings. The skillet provides the dry, even heat the dumplings need for a crisp crust and a juicy inside. We like to make this dessert in August when peaches are in full glory.

• • ● • •

MAKES 8 SERVINGS

4 peaches

Pastry
3 tablespoons sour cream
1/3 cup ice water
1 cup all-purpose flour
1/4 cup cornmeal
2 teaspoons sugar
1/2 teaspoon salt
7 tablespoons cold, unsalted butter, cut into 8 pieces

Sauce
3/4 cup dark brown sugar
1 1/2 cups water
1/4 cup (1/2 stick) butter
1/2 teaspoon ground cinnamon
1/4 cup granulated sugar

Nutmeg Cream
1 cup chilled half-and-half
1/4 cup granulated sugar
1 teaspoon freshly grated nutmeg

● Position a rack in the center of the oven and preheat to 375°F. Peel the peaches and cut them in half. Discard the pits.

● To prepare the pastry dough, whisk together the sour cream and ice water (removing the ice first) in a small bowl. Set aside.

• Place the flour, cornmeal, sugar, and salt in a large bowl. Mix with a whisk or fingers until well combined. Add the butter. Mix with your fingers, with a pastry knife, or in a food processor until you have pea-sized pieces of butter (if using a food processor, quickly pulse 8 times). Add the sour cream mixture 1 tablespoon at a time, gently mixing in after each addition. Once all the liquid has been added, form the dough into a large disk. Do not handle the dough too much, and work quickly so that the butter stays cold. Wrap with plastic wrap and refrigerate for 1 to 2 hours.

• To prepare the dumplings, roll out the chilled dough on a lightly floured surface until you have a 12- to 14-inch rectangle. With a sharp knife, cut the dough into 8 squares. Place a peach half in the middle of each square, bring the corners together, and pinch to seal. Try to enclose the fruit completely.

• To prepare the sauce, place the brown sugar, water, and butter in a 10-inch cast iron skillet and boil for 5 minutes over medium-high heat. Place the dumplings in the skillet with the sauce. Sprinkle the tops with the cinnamon and sugar. Place the skillet in the oven and bake for 30 minutes, until dumplings are lightly browned and you see juices beginning to leak out of the dumplings.

• While the dumplings are baking, prepare the Nutmeg Cream by combining the half-and-half, sugar, and nutmeg in a small bowl. Refrigerate until ready to serve.

• Remove the dumplings from the oven, set each on a plate, and serve with the chilled Nutmeg Cream.

CARDAMOM-APRICOT FINANCIER

A financier is a French almond cake. Our good friend Jeremy Faber inspired this delicious recipe. He made individual financiers with an apricot dropped in the center of each and served them with cardamom ice cream. The flavors were so incredible that we added the cardamom directly to the cake and achieved a perfect crust by making one large cake in the cast iron skillet. Serve with vanilla ice cream.

• • ● • •

MAKES 6 SERVINGS

1 cup slivered almonds
1⅔ cups powdered sugar
½ cup all-purpose flour
2 teaspoons ground cardamom
¼ teaspoon salt
Finely grated zest of 1 orange
6 large egg whites, lightly beaten (just until foamy)
¾ cup (1½ sticks) unsalted butter, melted
2 tablespoons unsalted butter for the pan
8 small apricots, halved and pitted

• • • • •

Powdered sugar, for serving
Vanilla ice cream, for serving

● Place the almonds in a cast iron skillet and toast over medium heat until light brown. Using a food processor, pulse the almonds until finely ground. In a large bowl, combine the ground almonds, powdered sugar, flour, cardamom, salt, and orange zest. Whisk in the egg whites. Slowly stir in the ¾ cup melted butter. Cover the bowl with plastic wrap and chill the batter in the refrigerator for 1 to 2 hours. (If you don't have this much time, you can instead place it in the freezer for 20 minutes.)

● Position a rack in the center of the oven and preheat to 450°F.

**THE
CAST IRON
SKILLET
COOKBOOK**

• Melt the 2 tablespoons butter over medium-low heat in a 10-inch cast iron skillet. Tilt the pan to coat the bottom and sides. Pour the batter into the skillet and drop the apricot halves on top (they will sink into the batter). Place the skillet in the oven and bake until the dough just begins to rise, about 10 minutes. Reduce the heat to 400°F and continue baking until the cake begins to brown around the edges and on top, 7 to 8 minutes longer.

• Turn off the oven and let the cake stand in the oven until firm, about 10 minutes. Transfer the pan to a wire rack to cool completely.

• Invert the financier onto the wire rack. Reinvert it onto a platter and slice into wedges. Dust with powdered sugar and serve with vanilla ice cream.

BREAD PUDDING WITH GRAND MARNIER SAUCE

The top of this bread pudding gets perfect, crusty little peaks; the inside is soft and custardy. You can make this a day ahead and bake it while you are having dinner. Serve warm with the Grand Marnier Sauce.

• • • • •

MAKES 8 SERVINGS

Bread Pudding

6 tablespoons (¾ stick) unsalted butter, divided

1 large French baguette or 10 slices French bread, cut into 1- to 2-inch cubes

½ cup raisins or dried cranberries, such as Craisins (optional)

⅔ cup chopped pecans (optional)

2 cups peeled, diced apples (Jonagold or Fuji)

3 large eggs

2 cups whole milk

1 cup half-and-half

1 cup sugar

1 tablespoon vanilla extract

3 tablespoons Grand Marnier

⅛ teaspoon ground cinnamon

⅛ teaspoon freshly grated nutmeg

⅛ teaspoon ground allspice

Grand Marnier Sauce

6 tablespoons (¾ stick) unsalted butter

¾ cup sugar

¼ cup Grand Marnier

1 egg

• • • • •

⅛ teaspoon freshly grated nutmeg, for serving

To prepare the bread pudding, butter a 10- or 12-inch cast iron skillet with 2 tablespoons of the butter. Layer half of the bread cubes, half of the raisins (if using), half of the chopped pecans (if using), and half of the apples in the skillet. Repeat with the remaining bread cubes, raisins, pecans, and apples.

In a large bowl, beat the 3 eggs until frothy. Add the milk, half-and-half, sugar, vanilla, Grand Marnier, cinnamon, nutmeg, and allspice. Whisk until well blended. Pour the egg mixture over the bread mixture in the skillet. Refrigerate for 1 hour, occasionally pressing down on the mixture gently to soak the bread cubes. Leave the bread cubes on top just lightly soaked with the egg mixture so that they will get slightly crispy when baked. Top the pudding with the remaining 4 tablespoons butter, cut into small pieces and distributed evenly over the top.

Position a rack in the center of the oven and preheat to 325°F. Place the skillet in the oven and bake for 1 hour. Remove from the oven and let cool for 30 minutes.

While the bread pudding is cooling, prepare the Grand Marnier Sauce. Melt the butter in a heavy saucepan over medium heat. Add the sugar and cook, stirring constantly with a wooden spoon, until the sugar has dissolved, about 2 minutes. Whisk in the Grand Marnier and cook for 1 to 2 minutes more. Remove from the heat.

In a medium bowl, whisk the egg until frothy. Stir ¼ cup of the Grand Marnier mixture into the egg, then add the egg mixture to the Grand Marnier mixture in the saucepan. Return the pan to low heat and cook, whisking, until the sauce begins to thicken, about 5 minutes.

Sprinkle the ground nutmeg over the bread pudding, then cut the pudding into wedges and serve with the warm sauce. (You can pour the sauce over the top or serve it on the side.)

APPLE CAKE WITH CARAMEL FROSTING AND CHOPPED PECANS

With its rich caramel frosting, this cake has the flavor of caramel apples. It's so easy to prepare; everything is mixed together in one bowl, then baked, frosted, and served in the cast iron skillet.

• • • • •

MAKES 8 SERVINGS

2$\frac{1}{3}$ cups all-purpose flour
2 cups granulated sugar
2 teaspoons baking soda
$\frac{1}{2}$ teaspoon salt
1 teaspoon ground cinnamon
$\frac{1}{4}$ teaspoon ground nutmeg
4 cups peeled, grated apple (about 1$\frac{1}{2}$ pounds)
$\frac{1}{2}$ cup vegetable shortening
2 eggs

Caramel Frosting
$\frac{1}{3}$ cup butter
$\frac{1}{2}$ cup light brown sugar
3 tablespoons whole milk
$\frac{1}{2}$ teaspoon vanilla extract
1$\frac{1}{2}$ cups powdered sugar

• • • • • •

$\frac{1}{2}$ cup chopped pecans, for serving

● Position a rack in the center of the oven and preheat to 350°F. Butter a 10-inch cast iron skillet, dust with flour, and tap out the excess.

● To make the cake, combine the flour, sugar, baking soda, salt, cinnamon, and nutmeg in a large bowl and mix well. Add the apples, shortening, and eggs to the flour mixture and beat with an electric mixer on medium speed until well blended. The batter will be stiff. Spread the batter evenly in the skillet.

● Bake until a toothpick inserted in the center of the cake comes out clean, 40 to 45 minutes. Cool in the pan.

● To make the frosting, melt the butter in a small saucepan over medium heat. Add the brown sugar and stir until the sugar dissolves. Add the milk and bring to a boil. Pour into a mixing bowl and let cool for 10 minutes. Add the vanilla extract and powdered sugar and beat with a whisk until creamy. (The frosting will thicken as it cools.) Spread evenly over the cooled apple cake. Sprinkle the chopped pecans over the top, and serve.

BING CHERRY CLAFOUTI

Clafouti is a French dessert similar to a Dutch baby but thicker and custard-like. It puffs up and gets golden in the skillet, and the cherries stay moist and sweet. We like to serve it for dessert or for a late weekend breakfast, warm with powdered sugar sprinkled over the top. Frozen Bing cherries, already pitted, make this a year-round favorite. We also like to substitute fresh apricots, pitted and quartered.

• • ● • •

MAKES 6 SERVINGS

2 cups (one 10-ounce package) frozen Bing cherries, thawed in a colander
1¼ cups all-purpose flour
⅓ cup granulated sugar
2¼ cups whole milk
4 eggs, lightly beaten
1 teaspoon vanilla extract
2 teaspoons Kirsch (cherry liqueur, optional)
¼ teaspoon freshly grated nutmeg
Zest of 1 orange
1 tablespoon butter, cut into small pieces

• • ● • •

Powdered sugar, for garnish

● Position a rack in the center of the oven and preheat to 400°F.

● Butter the bottom and sides of a 12-inch cast iron skillet. Place the cherries in the bottom of the pan, distributing evenly. In a medium bowl, mix the flour and sugar. Whisk in the milk, mixing until combined. Add the eggs, vanilla, Kirsch (if using), nutmeg, and orange zest. Whisk until well combined. Pour all of the batter over the top of the cherries in the skillet. Dot the top with butter.

● Place the skillet in the oven and bake until puffed and golden, 25 to 30 minutes. Sprinkle with powdered sugar and serve.

SKILLET BAKED APPLES

You know you are about to enjoy a relaxing and comfortable meal when you walk into a friend's home and spot a skillet of apples waiting to be baked. By the end of dinner, the smell of baking apples fills the air.

• • ● • •

MAKES 8 SERVINGS

8 Jonagold apples, cored and peel removed 1 inch around the top
6 tablespoons (¾ stick) butter, at room temperature
1 cup light brown sugar
24 small marshmallows
½ cup chilled heavy cream

• • ● • •

Chopped candied walnuts, for garnish

Position a rack in the center of the oven and preheat to 375°F.

Place the apples in a 10- or 12-inch cast iron skillet. Mix the butter and brown sugar in a small bowl. Place 3 marshmallows in the bottom of each apple (this will keep the filling from running out of the apple). Place 2 tablespoons of the butter mixture in the center of each apple. Bake for 40 minutes. Serve warm in shallow dessert dishes with the chilled heavy cream poured around the apples. Sprinkle with the candied walnuts.

PLUM GALETTE

A galette is a free-form tart. You roll out the pastry and then fold the edges over the fruit. Served in the cast iron skillet, this rustic dessert, with its golden crust and shiny, glazed plums, makes a beautiful presentation at the table.

• • ● • •

MAKES 6 TO 8 SERVINGS

Pastry

1/3 cup sour cream

1/2 cup ice-cold water

1 1/2 cups all-purpose flour

1/3 cup yellow cornmeal

3 teaspoons sugar, plus 1 tablespoon for sprinkling on the pre-baked dough

1/2 teaspoon salt

10 tablespoons chilled unsalted butter, cut into 8 pieces

Filling

20 Italian plums, halved and pitted, or 10 of the larger variety plums, quartered

1/2 cup sugar

2 tablespoons cornstarch

2 teaspoons fresh lemon juice

Glaze

5 tablespoons plum jam or marmalade

3 tablespoons water

1 tablespoon Grand Marnier or rum

• • ● • •

Vanilla ice cream or whipped cream, for serving

● To prepare the pastry, whisk together the sour cream and ice water in a small bowl. Set aside.

Place the flour, cornmeal, the 3 teaspoons sugar, and salt in a large bowl. Mix with a dry whisk or your fingers until well blended. Add the butter. Mix with your hands or a pastry blender, or in a food processor until the pieces of butter are pea-sized (about 8 to 10 pulses in the food processor). Add the sour cream mixture, 1 tablespoon at a time, gently mixing after each addition. Once all the liquid has been added, form the dough into a large disk. Don't handle the dough too much, and work quickly so that the butter stays cold. Wrap with plastic wrap and refrigerate for 1 to 2 hours.

To prepare the filling, while the dough is chilling, place the plums in a large bowl with the sugar, cornstarch, and lemon juice.

Position a rack in the center of the oven and preheat to 400°F.

To prepare the glaze, place the jam, water, and Grand Marnier in a small saucepan. Bring to a gentle boil over medium-low heat. Remove from the heat and set aside.

To prepare the galette, roll out the chilled dough on a lightly floured surface until you have a 14- to 16-inch circle. Lightly flour the top of the dough. Fold the dough over the rolling pin and transfer to an 8-inch cast iron skillet. Gently press the dough into the bottom and against the sides of the skillet. It just needs to stick to the sides while you add the filling. Arrange the plums in the pan in a circular pattern, slightly overlapping one another, skin side up, starting at the outer edges and working toward the center. Quickly reheat glaze and spoon over the plums. Fold the edges of the pastry over the fruit. It will form pleats, and that's the result you want. You should have a roughly 2- to 3-inch border of dough folded in all around the edges. Sprinkle the plums and crust with the 1 tablespoon sugar. Bake until the crust is golden brown, 25 to 30 minutes. Serve in the skillet with vanilla ice cream or whipped cream.

CARAMELIZED APPLE AND GINGERBREAD CAKE

Actually an upside-down cake, this gingerbread is light, fluffy, and incredibly moist. Cooking the apples this way creates a lovely caramel sauce for the top of the cake. The Whipped Eggnog Cream complements the cake.

• • ● • •

MAKES 8 TO 10 SERVINGS

Caramelized Apples

5 tablespoons unsalted butter, cut into 8 pieces
⅔ cup granulated sugar
3 apples (Gala, Fuji, or Golden Delicious), peeled, cored, and cut into
  1-inch wedges

Gingerbread Cake

1½ cups water
½ cup molasses
½ cup maple syrup
1 teaspoon baking soda
½ cup (1 stick) unsalted butter, at room temperature
1 cup light brown sugar
1 large egg
2½ cups all-purpose flour
½ teaspoon salt
1 tablespoon baking powder
2 teaspoons ground ginger
1 teaspoon ground cinnamon
¼ teaspoon ground or freshly grated nutmeg

Whipped Eggnog Cream

½ cup heavy cream
½ cup eggnog

● To prepare the apples, melt the butter and sugar in a 10-inch cast iron skillet over medium-low heat. Do not stir. When the mixture begins to caramelize, in about 15 to 20 minutes, remove the pan from the heat and allow it to cool slightly. Arrange the apples in the skillet in a circular

pattern, starting from the outer edge and working toward the center. Return the skillet to medium-low heat and cook the apples for 10 minutes. Remove from the heat and set aside.

- To prepare the cake, bring the water to a boil in a medium saucepan. Remove from the heat and add the molasses, maple syrup, and baking soda. Stir, and set aside to cool.

- Mix the butter and brown sugar in a large bowl, using an electric mixer, until light and fluffy. Add the egg and beat for another 5 to 10 seconds.

- In a separate bowl, sift together the flour, salt, baking powder, ginger, cinnamon, and nutmeg. Using an electric mixer on low speed, add the flour mixture to the butter and brown sugar mixture in thirds, alternating with the molasses mixture. After all the wet and dry ingredients have been added, continue mixing on low speed until all of the lumps are gone and the batter is smooth. Do not overmix.

- Pour the cake batter over the top of the apples in the skillet, being careful not to disturb the apples. Bake until a toothpick comes out clean when inserted in the center of the cake, 30 to 35 minutes. Remove from the oven and let rest for 5 minutes. Run a butter knife around the outside edge of the cake to loosen it. Place a large plate on top of the skillet and, using hot pads, grasp the plate and skillet tightly. Invert the cake onto the plate. Rearrange the apples if any have stuck to the skillet.

- To prepare the Whipped Eggnog Cream, beat the heavy cream and eggnog with an electric mixer until stiff. Serve the cake topped with eggnog cream.

RESOURCES

Bob's Red Mill Natural Foods, Inc.
5209 SE International Way
Milwaukie, OR 97222
503-654-3215
www.bobsredmill.com
Grains, cornmeal

Tom Douglas's Rubs with Love
206-441-4122
www.tomdouglas.com
Spice rubs

Lodge Manufacturing Company
P.O. Box 380
South Pittsburg, TN 37380
423-837-7181
www.lodgemfg.com
Our preferred supplier of cast iron cookware

Mama Lil's
206-726-8372
www.mamalils.com
Pickled Hungarian goathorn peppers

More Than Gourmet
800-860-9385
www.morethangourmet.com
Demi-glaces, stocks, and other sauces

The Spanish Table
1427 Western Avenue
Seattle, WA 98101
206-682-2827
www.spanishtable.com
Spanish olive oils, smoked paprika, and specialty ingredients

Staub USA, Inc.
115 Pine Avenue, Suite 640
Long Beach, CA 90802
866-782-8287
www.staubusa.com
Beautiful and unique cast iron pieces from France

Sur la Table
84 Pine Street
Seattle, WA 98101
800-243-0852
www.surlatable.com
Staub and Le Creuset cast iron pieces for cooking and serving, splatter guard, cast iron handle mitts, and a large range of cookware

Washington State University Creamery
101 Food Quality Building
P.O. Box 641122
Pullman, WA 99161-1122
800-457-5442
Cougar Gold cheese

World Spice Merchants
1509 Western Avenue
Seattle, WA 98101
206-682-7274
www.worldspice.com
Fresh spices and spice blends

INDEX

HARKER HEARNE

Sharon Kramis (above, right) is the author of two cookbooks, *Northwest Bounty* and *Berries: A Country Garden Cookbook*. A Northwest native, she holds a degree in food science from the University of Washington and is a former food writer for the *Mercer Island Reporter*. Sharon studied with legendary cooking figure James Beard at his summer cooking school in Seaside, Oregon, for six years. She is a founding member of the International Association of Culinary Professionals, Les Dames d'Escoffier's Seattle chapter, and FareStart, a program that trains homeless persons for the hospitality industry. In addition to participating in menu development for Anthony's Restaurants in Seattle, Sharon continues to educate herself through travel and ongoing classes at the California Culinary Academy in Napa Valley. She lives with her husband, Larry, in Seattle.

ABOUT THE AUTHORS

Julie Kramis Hearne (above, left) was brought up with a love for food. When she was young, she would pretend to be sick so she could stay home from school and watch her mother teach cooking classes, and she often accompanied her mother to James Beard's cooking classes. The former owner of two Seattle restaurants, Julie has worked as a restaurant consultant and spent a year learning at the nationally renowned Herbfarm Restaurant in Woodinville, Washington. Julie is a member of Women Chefs and Restaurateurs, the International Association of Culinary Professionals, and Women for Wine Sense, and is currently on the board of Slow Food. She continues to learn about food through ongoing classes at the California Culinary Academy in Napa Valley. She lives with her husband, Harker, and two young sons in Seattle.